MISSIONAL VIBRANCY
AND
FINANCIAL VIABILITY

Alternative Financial Models for Churches and Church Plants When Tithes and Offerings Are Not Enough

W. JAY MOON

Missional Vibrancy and Financial Viability
Copyright © 2021 by W. Jay Moon

Exponential is a growing movement of activists committed to the multiplication of healthy new churches. Exponential Resources spotlights actionable principles, ideas and solutions for the accelerated multiplication of healthy, reproducing faith communities. For more information, visit exponential.org.

All rights reserved. No part of this book, including icons and images, may be reproduced in any manner without prior written permission from copyright holder, except where noted in the text and in the case of brief quotations embodied in critical articles and reviews.

Unless otherwise indicated, all Scripture quotations are taken from the Holy Bible, New International Version, copyright ©1973, 1978, 1984, 2011 by International Bible Society. All emphases in Scripture quotations have been added by the author.

Scriptures marked NLT are taken from the New Living Translation Copyright ©1996, 2004, 2007. Used by permission of Tyndale House Publishers, Inc., Carol Stream, Illinois 60188.

Scriptures marked ESV are taken from The Holy Bible, English Standard Version® (ESV®) Copyright © 2001 by Crossway, a publishing ministry of Good News Publishers. All rights reserved.

ISBN 13-978-1-62424-059-1 (eBook)
ISBN 13-978-1-62424-060-7 (Print)

Cover and interior design by Harrington Interactive Media (harringtoninteractive.com)

This book is manufactured in the United States.

Inside

Foreword by Dr. Mark DeYmaz 5

CHAPTER 1 Changing Financial Picture 9

CHAPTER 2 We Have Options 21

CHAPTER 3 Monetizing Existing
Church Assets 29

CHAPTER 4 Incubating New Businesses 35

CHAPTER 5 Non-Profits Form Mission Arms
of the Church 47

CHAPTER 6 Co-Vocational Pastoring Opens
Multiple Income Streams 53

CHAPTER 7 Entrepreneurial Churches Locate
Church Inside the Marketplace 59

CHAPTER 8 Decentralized Churches 77

CHAPTER 9 Cautions to Consider 81

CHAPTER 10 Your Turn! 89

Appendix 97
Notes 99
Bibliography 113
About the Author 119

FOREWORD

By Dr. Mark DeYmaz

Since orchestrating Little Rock's historic Racial Reconciliation Rally in 1997 (together with the late Greg Mirtha), planting the Mosaic Church of Central Arkansas in 2001, and establishing the Mosaix Global Network with Dr. George Yancey in 2004, I have been widely recognized as a champion of the now firmly established yet still maturing Multiethnic Church Movement. The fact is, I continue to devote much of my life and work to helping ministry leaders, local churches, Christian schools and non-profits build healthy multiethnic and economically diverse, socially just, and culturally intelligent organizations. My passion is to advance a credible gospel in an increasingly diverse, painfully polarized, and cynical society.

With the publication of my book (co-authored with my colleague of nineteen years, Dr. Harry Li), *The Coming Revolution in Church Economics* (Baker Books, 2019), however, an entirely new field of inquiry, discussion, and possibilities was launched in the American Church. The work makes the theological, sociological, and practical case for why tithes and offerings, alone, will no longer be enough to fund bold ministry in a rapidly changing world. Therefore, and since its publication, I too have been blessed to form an entirely new set of professional associations and personal relationships, having been sought out or introduced to other disruptive innovators, entrepreneurial outliers, and like-minded practitioners championing the same cause, for similar reasons, within their own spheres of influence.

Jay Moon is one of those people.

Having spent time with Jay, having heard him speak, and having examined his work, I can assure you: behind the words he writes herein are proven, credible, and ongoing works that back them up. Indeed, Jay is a quintessential renaissance man. A lifetime's pursuit of varying interests, experiences, and understanding today allows him to navigate effortlessly and effectively across an otherwise erroneous sacred-secular divide. He is at once adept on the mission field and in the marketplace; behind a pulpit or a pint; in working with scholars, students, current customers or potential clients. In short, his directional advice can be trusted.

That's why I'm honored to introduce Jay to you and excited for you to read this book, his latest, outlining "alternative financial models for churches and church plants."

In the future, pastors and church planters will need to do much more than solicit donations, host Financial Peace University, preach yet another sermon on generosity, or chase numeric growth to ensure the financial stability, let alone sustainability, of the churches they seek to plant, grow or develop. Toward that end, we must learn to leverage congregational assets to bless the community, create multiple streams of income, and generate sustainable revenue . . . in short, to embrace the principles and practices of Church Economics.

Only in so doing can we hope to ensure the "missional vibrancy and financial viability" of our churches long-term . . . the churches we love and daily labor to establish, in fulfillment of our calling, for the sake of the gospel.

Dr. Mark DeYmaz

Founding Pastor & Directional Leader, Mosaic Church of Central Arkansas

Co-founder & CEO, Mosaix Global Network

CHAPTER 1
Changing Financial Picture

Churches are closing at an alarming rate. Thom Rainer estimates that 16,000 churches in the U.S. may shutter their doors and turn off the lights for the last time in 2021.[1] It pains me to hear this, particularly when several of these churches are closed due to financial reasons that could have been avoided.

For example, Highland Heights Baptist Church in Memphis, TN dwindled in size from its glory days of several hundred people to only twenty-five active members, resulting in the plummeting of tithes and offerings.[2] If a big expenditure arises such as a leaky roof or water boiler failure, then the church will not know where to turn since their tithes and offerings cannot cover these expenses. Three aging churches, nearby to Highland Heights, have already closed due to similar problems. The remaining few people scattered throughout the large worship space are silently asking themselves, "When will we need to close our doors?"

Church planting teams have a similar problem. They are passionate about their vision but after several months of difficult fundraising, it is not uncommon for the team leader to silently ask, "Will we ever raise the money that we need to get this church started?" Common church planting financial models ask the planting team to raise money up front for the first three years' budget prior to planting – that amounts to $300,000 - $500,000 on average for a church plant in the U.S.[3] How many teams can raise this amount of money? Even more critical, how many more churches could be planted if this limitation was eliminated?

Both examples are all too common in the North American church context. Even if we take more conservative estimates, about 4,000 churches will likely close this year. There are various reasons behind the closures, but financial concerns are often an important consideration. In addition, about 4,000 churches will likely be planted this year.[4] Many will not survive due to financial considerations. Many more could also be planted if there were other financial approaches.

OUTDATED FINANCIAL MODELS

Mark DeYmaz and Harry Li (2019), in their book *The Coming Revolution in Church Economics,* warn that the financial models of many American churches will not be sustainable into the future. The Boomer and Builder generations are responsible for most of the church giving presently. As they age, the generations behind them are not only attending church less but they are often more prone to tipping instead of tithing. This is reflected in less giving as percentage of income to the American church (even while giving to charitable causes overall has risen slightly).[5] While the church has benefited from property tax exemption and clergy housing credits, there has been talk in recent years of these benefits being rescinded, particularly as governments are looking for ways to support the social services voters are requesting.[6] DeYmaz and Li conclude that tithes and offerings will no longer be enough to financially support many churches in the 21st century based on the reductions described above in church attendance, giving, and tax exemptions.[7] Many church planters and pastors are pondering what other options exist when the tithes/offerings model (that worked for so long) is no longer viable into the future.

CURSE OF KNOWLEDGE

Doug Paul in his book *Kingdom Innovation* noted that churches can fall into the same trap as businesses called the curse of knowledge. In short, when a business is suffering losses, they tend to double down on what 'worked' in the past. The knowledge of previous success then becomes a curse that prevents them for trying new options. For example, there was a time when families made a weekend ritual of going to Blockbuster to check out a video to watch. When Blockbuster started to lose market share to digital providers, Blockbuster largely doubled down on what they knew best - provide hard copies of videos. This previous success in the analogue world prevented them from making the shift to the digital world. Unfortunately, it led Blockbuster to bankruptcy and eventual closure.

Churches can fall into the same trap. When faced with decline, pastors and church planters cannot see other options since they are 'cursed' by their previous success. Wharton business school professor Adam Grant describes it this way in his book *Originals*, "The more expertise and experience people gain, the more entrenched they become in a particular way of viewing the world. . . . As we gain knowledge about a domain, we become prisoners of our prototypes" (2016, p. 78). Even the most successful and experienced church planters and pastors then can become 'prisoners of their own prototypes.'

Is your church operating in a Blockbuster world when the surrounding context is moving toward a Netflix world? Many pastors and church planters recognize that the traditional financial options are working less and less but the curse of knowledge prevents them from seeing or trying other financial models.

COVID

Then the COVID pandemic hit in 2020 when churches went on lock down for weeks and even months. For those churches that did not have online giving in place, many suffered financial setbacks, making it hard to recover. According to Jim Tomberlin and Warren Bird, who wrote the book *Better Together: Making Church Mergers Work*, just over 25% of the churches in America are somewhere between death and life support. These churches are simply not sure if they will be able to keep the doors open much longer. The COVID pandemic exposed the financial weaknesses of many churches. As a result, the pandemic served to accelerate the existing trajectory – they were struggling with finances before the pandemic and this simply was the last straw to put some churches over the edge.[8]

Many church plants were hit even harder by the pandemic. Without cash reserves and a steady cash flow that more established churches may have, the planter often does not know where to turn. Elizabeth Rios, executive director for Plant4Harvest, an organization that coaches and trains black and Latino faith leaders to start multiethnic churches in urban communities commented, "This has the potential to wipe out church plants."[9] While still full of vision and hope, these church planters wonder if there is another financial approach to fulfill the dreams God has given them.

GOOD NEWS

I have some good news for you. There are other options to finance your church or church plant! This book will expose you to these alternative financial models that can change the financial picture of your church or church plant. Too many times, churches are relying upon outdated church financial models that are not viable in the 21st century. I will describe six non-traditional financial options for you to consider for your own church or church plant. My hope is that you will find one or more of these models that will be ideally suited for your context. As you try these approaches, you will find renewed financial viability as well as missional vibrancy.

Instead of a "one size fits all" approach, we will explore various approaches to identify one that fits the financial picture at your church or church plant. I will share important factors to determine which option is most suitable at your own church. In addition, I will provide contemporary examples to demonstrate that this is not simply wishful thinking; rather, existing churches and church plants are already utilizing these approaches, resulting in both financial health and missional impact. In addition, I will provide some cautions to consider when dealing with money so that we employ money as a good servant and not allow it to become a bad master.

DOCTOR'S CHECKUP

Since you are reading this book, I am assuming that you already recognize the financial model that relies upon tithes and offerings alone is not going to cut it for your church/church plant. You recognize the problem, and you are looking for solutions. Like going to your doctor for a checkup on your blood pressure, heartbeat and temperature, the journey to discuss church finances will begin with a reality check that does not mince words; rather, it gets quickly to the heart of the matter.

Your first step will be to take a few moments to do a checkup. Then, we can do a further diagnosis for your next steps toward church financial health. While we will talk a lot about finances in this book, it is paramount that you are motivated by two factors – missional vibrancy and financial viability. In other words, the financial health of your church is not simply to keep the lights on; rather, this is to allow your church to have an impact on the lives of those in the community and give you capacity to witness in word and deeds. In short, money is a good servant but a bad master. As a result, the goal of this book is to strengthen your church's financial position so that you will have greater capacity for mission.

If you have compassion but not capacity, then you will be frustrated. If you have compassion *and* capacity, then you can be transformative. Like the story of the good Samaritan in Luke 15, Pastor Tom Nelson (2017) speculates that the Levite and Pharisee likely had compassion for the injured traveler, but they did not have capacity to help. On the other hand, the Samaritan had compassion and capacity. Note how the Samaritan basically gave the equivalent of a credit card to the inn keeper to take care of the injured traveler until he returned. In other words, he had capacity to help that matched his compassion, resulting in a transformed life.

Likewise, my prayer for you is that you will dig into the financial matters at your church/church plant with gusto since this can provide capacity to match your compassion. Contrary to popular opinion, the topic of money is not simply a secular discussion; rather, a godly understanding and use of money can be used to create great spiritual transformation.[10] As a result, I encourage you to roll up your sleeves and dig into the financial nuts and bolts of church planting so that these financial models can be regarded as good servants to empower the church to fulfill her mission.

Much like the parable of the talents, many churches are simply sitting on their underutilized talents. The word "profit" (when earned in a godly manner) is not a dirty word; rather, the Lord is pleased when five talents are turned into ten and angered when the one talent is buried (Matthew 25:14-30). What could happen if churches stopped sitting on their assets and considered other financial approaches?

This book is written for practitioners. At the end of each chapter, you are invited into practice exercises. These are meant to help you evaluate your own church's finances and develop an initial plan towards financial health. The exercises get you started in considering alternative financial models for your church or church plant. These are best done in a small group within your church or church planting team, but they can also be done alone. Just don't skip over them.

PRACTICE

Doctor's Physical: To get started, obtain a copy of your annual budget, giving amounts for the last year (or projected giving for your church plant), and church's mission statement. Discuss the following:

1. What is the overall feeling about the financial health of your church or church plant?

   - Are people positive or slowly losing hope?
   - Are people aware how their giving makes a difference in the community/world?
   - Do people respond to giving needs in the church OR do they give elsewhere?

2. Look at your church budget in one hand and your church's mission statement in the other:

   - Are there any expenses that do not further the mission statement of your church that can be eliminated?
   - Are there other expenses that have simply been added onto the budget but do not serve a vital purpose anymore? Ask, "If I removed this item, would the mission of the church suffer?"
   - Trim the budget to meet the missional purpose of your church or church plant.

3. Look at the trend of giving in your church:

   - Is the direction toward more giving or less over the last few years?
   - Are the donors at risk of discontinuing their giving (e.g., elderly, job at risk, potential move or life change)?
   - If online giving is not available, can this be added so that people can set up automatic giving?

4. Compare the monthly giving to the monthly expenses:

   - Is the church able to meet the budget?
   - If not, how much shortfall is there?
   - If yes, how much money is saved in the bank?

5. Calculate the number of months the church can stay open with no income:

   - Divide the amount in savings by the monthly budget amount. That will indicate how many months the church can operate without income. A good target number is three months for a healthy church.[11]
   E.g., Savings = $30,000. Monthly budget = $10,000.
   Months to stay open without income = $30,000/$10,000/mo. = 3 months.

6. Determine the following ratios from the yearly budget:

   - (Salary & Benefits)/total budget. This is obtained by adding the salaries and benefits of all staff and dividing by the total budget. The accounting firm CapinCrouse recommends that financially healthy churches often have a number between 40-55%.[12]
   - Debt/total budget. The debt is obtained by adding the amount paid for the building mortgage to any other outstanding debt payments (land, equipment, etc.). CapinCrouse recommends that the ratio of debt/total budget for healthy churches is less than 15%.
   - (Personnel costs + Debt payments)/total budget. CapinCrouse recommends that this number should be between 40-70% for a healthy church.

7. Review the above checkup. Discuss the following with your team:

   - Which of the above financial numbers is your church/church plant's strongest area?
   - Which of the above financial numbers is your church/church plant's weakest area?

- What changes may you need to consider to personnel or the building due to the above ratios?
- What ministry areas is the church/church plant most known for in the community? I.e., what would the community miss the most if the church were not there?
- What possible ministry areas would the church love to participate in if there were more financial capacity? I.e., what area of passion would your church engage if you had more capacity?

CHAPTER 2
We Have Options

How will pastors and church planters, who are called by God, find sufficient finances to support themselves and their churches?[13] I developed the acronym "MINCE" to describe five non-traditional approaches that churches may use to weather the financial storms. This acronym also describes how I will not mince words when talking about finances; instead, I want to be clear and straight to the point considering the following five approaches:

1. **M**onetize[14] existing church assets
2. **I**ncubate new businesses
3. **N**on-profits form mission arms of the church
4. **C**o-vocational pastoring opens multiple income streams
5. **E**ntrepreneurial churches locate church inside the marketplace

Each of these approaches can more effectively utilize the assets already available to the church.

In short, these non-traditional approaches can greatly reduce the number of church closures and increase the number of church plants. Research over the last five years with churches that are using these non-traditional financial approaches in the U.S. and abroad demonstrate that these methods are working! This is not simply wishful thinking. Like any movement, there are some that are ahead of the learning curve, and we will lean into their wisdom and experience, drawing widely from Mark DeYmaz and Harry Li's book mentioned above since they are among those pastor/church planters that are already implementing these changes.[15]

CONTEXT SPECIFIC FACTORS

To start off, there is no silver bullet. Simply put, each church needs to consider their context to determine which approach is best (as you will do in the practice section to follow). To help understand the most favorable context for each approach, two variables, Financial Liquidity and Access to Relational Networks, interact to create appropriate contexts for different financial approaches (see Figure 2.1). These variables will be described and then related to the financial approaches used by churches.

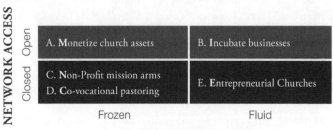

Figure 2.1. Access to Relational Networks vs. Position of Financial Liquidity

Financial Liquidity: From a business standpoint (Mueller, 2019), "Financial liquidity refers to how easily assets can be converted into cash. Assets like stocks and bonds are very liquid since they can be converted to cash within days. However, large assets such as property, plant, and equipment are not as easily converted to cash." A church may have a range of asset types available, between cash being scarce (or tied up in a building or land) to cash being readily available. A church's financial assets may be frozen (with limited access to cash), often leading to a scarcity mentality and low risk taking. On the other hand, a church's financial assets may be more fluid such that there is an abundance mentality with access to cash, and entrepreneurial thinking. In Figure 2.1, the x axis considers the present financial position of the church/church plant, from frozen to fluid. The y axis considers the church's access to relational networks, from closed to open.

Relational Networks: When researching how people came to faith, Win and Charles Arn (1988) found the vast majority (75-90 percent) came to church due to an invitation from a friend or family member.[16] These relational networks are crucial for church planters. Donald McGavran (1981) considered these relational networks of family and friends so important to church growth and health that he labeled them bridges of God. Church growth specialist, George Hunter (2009, p. 66) summarizes, "churches grow as they reach out across the social networks of their people, especially their newest converts…" When these relational networks are still open, there is frequent and easy access to discussions between church members and those outside the church. Relational networks can close, however, due to several reasons such as moving, interpersonal conflicts, and neglect. One reason networks close is when new Christians stop socializing with their old friends.[17] There is a range whereby churches have access to their relational networks. At one end of the continuum, some churches have closed access to networks of people they can contact and invite to their church. On the other end of the continuum, churches maintain wide open access such that they regularly and freely engage people outside the church, in the neighborhood, at work, on social media, etc.

The real benefit of exploring church sustainability comes from the intersection of these two factors, indicating which of the MINCE approaches are most suitable as a starting point. These five approaches are not exclusive; rather, churches may use a combination of approaches. Figure 2.1 is simply meant to provide a starting point to help churches know where to begin the path of flourishing again.

In the following chapters, I will discuss each of these approaches (and add one more). To get started on deciding starting points for your own church/church plant, please spend time discussing the following practice questions.

PRACTICE

1. Relational networks: Consider the number of relationships that people in the church have with those that are unchurched or de-churched.[18] While this is hard to quantify, discuss with your church team the strength and quantity of relationships with unchurched or de-churched people. Discuss:

   - Do we know and spend time with people who are unchurched or de-churched?
   - List the names of people that you interact with at least monthly that are not going to a church. Pray for them by name and look for opportunities to love and serve them.
   - How many of these people do we know well enough to invite to an event or activity at the church?
   - For a church of 100 people:
     - Do you have 10–20 such relationships? If so, your church is in the network access category of "Open."
     - Do you have less than 10 such relationships? If so, your church is in the network access category of "Closed."
     - Use this result to find your church's position on the y-axis in Figure 2.2 (page 27).

2. Financial Liquidity: To find the church's position on the x-axis in Figure 2.2, you will determine the financial liquidity of the church using the quick ratio (QR).[19] The QR measures the ability of a church to use their liquid assets to meet their debt obligations, as shown in the following equation:

QR = (Cash + Marketable Securities + Pledges)/Current Liabilities

To plug in the appropriate numbers above, use the follow definitions:

- **Cash** = Cash available today
- **Marketable Securities** = Investments that can be quickly converted to cash, such as stocks, bonds, and money market funds
- **Pledges** (if applicable) = Some churches ask members to make a pledge for the year[20]
- **Current Liabilities** = Debts that need to be paid in the year (largely the rent or mortgage payment) For example, Home Church has cash savings of $20,000, investments in stock of $4,000, no yearly pledges, and yearly mortgage payments of $30,000.

   The QR calculation is:
   QR = ($20,000 + $4,000)/$30,000 = 0.8

- Is the QR > 1? If so, the church can meet their debt obligations and has extra money left over. Your church is in the Financial Liquidity category of "Fluid."

- Is the QR < 1? If so, the church is not able to meet their debt obligations. Your church is in the Financial Liquidity category of "Frozen."
- Use this result to find your church's position on the x-axis in Figure 2.2.

3. Now that you have identified your church's x and y positions in Figure 2.2, this indicates the first option to start exploring for an alternative financial model for your church. For example, Home Church is in quadrant A (QR = 0.8 and 20 relationships with unchurched and de-churched people in the community). Home church then should start looking at ways to monetize the church's existing assets, which we will explore further in the next chapter.

Figure 2.2 below will now be used for the remainder of the book to help you identify the best starting point for an alternative financial model for your church or church plant.

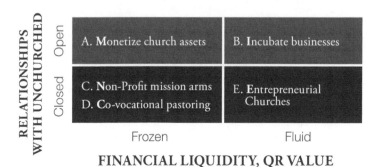

Figure 2.2. Number of Relationships with Unchurched People vs. Financial Liquidity (QR)

CHAPTER 3
Monetizing Existing Church Assets

Some churches have very little access to cash (liquidity is frozen), yet their relational networks are still strong and open (position A in Figure 2.2, top left). This means they still have access to people outside the church that interact with them and trust them. Highland Heights Baptist Church was in this position. As their attendance dwindled, so did the cash reserves. This was the opportune time for the church to recognize and then monetize their existing assets. For example, many churches heat and cool a building that is left empty most of the week. This building is a huge asset that can be monetized. In the process, it can provide an income stream as well as meet missional needs in the community.

CO-WORKING

Wilmore United Methodist Church recognized their building space was greatly under-utilized. At the same time, millennials in the gig economy were looking for work space. This has led to a movement of coworking spaces across the country whereby young entrepreneurs will rent a desk sometimes with access to a copier, board room, coffee machine, bathroom, and important relational connections. What could happen if churches filled this need and offered coworking space for rent? E. Mazareanu (2019) notes, "Coworking is a new but fast-growing trend in the United States - from only fourteen spaces in 2007, the number of coworking and other shared, collaborative office spaces increased to 4,043 in 2017." Several coworking companies have arisen to fill this need.[21] When Wilmore UMC was approached by some millennials with this need, twenty-three folks (largely seminary students) signed up. This not only provided an income stream for the church, but it also addressed a need of millennials that now recognized the church as relevant and engaged in their issues and concerns.

A number of churches are now opening their buildings for coworking space during the week. Svetlana Papazov (2019, p. 24) calls this a "church for Monday" since its missional purpose is to "close the perilous Sunday to Monday gap by uniting worship on Sunday to work on Monday." As a result, Real Life Church in Richmond, VA offers coworking spaces. Pastor Papazov, however, has taken this a step further by providing business and life coaching in the Real Life Center for Entrepreneurial and Leadership Excellence.

SHORT-TERM RENTAL

Consider the popularity of Airbnb among millennials who are looking for an experience as they travel.[22] Regarding this from a missional perspective, Airbnb challenges Christians to do what they should do - be hospitable. Airbnb incentivizes its hosts to practice hospitality by opening a room for short term rental. At the same time, Airbnb offers the opportunity to connect with others, treat them with kindness, and hopefully lead to faith discussions. Churches can open a parsonage or other space to travelers who are thankful for the accommodation. Again, this not only provides an income stream but also engages the church to meet the needs of the community via hospitality. The result can be a fresh missional engagement. My wife and I run an Airbnb at our house that has led to many faith discussions as well as some guests even coming to church with us.

These financial approaches are open to churches with limited cash since it usually requires very little funds to operate. Some entrepreneurs have seized this opportunity and will often gladly spend the money up front to re-arrange or repair space so it can be monetized in this way.[23]

PRACTICE:

Gather the leadership team of your church/church plant to discuss:

1. List the assets that God has given the church team to steward. To get started, consider the following possibilities (this list is not comprehensive):

   - Physical assets: Building, land, parking lot
   - Spiritual assets: What gifts, talents, abilities are in your church/church plant to produce spiritual capital? There may be people who are gifted in counseling, mentoring, teaching, etc.
   - Social assets: What gifts, talents, abilities are in your church/church plant to produce social capital? Particularly consider those that connect people to each other. Consider the daily jobs of those in your church or church plant since the marketplace is a fertile network of exchange where people create value for each other.

2. Read together the parable of the talents in Matthew 25:14-30 where God has given everyone at least one or more talents. Then discuss:

   - Which one of the three servants is most like our church/church plant?
   - What talents are we burying by not using?

- What opportunities exist to use these talents for kingdom purposes?
- God is pleased when we utilize all our talents to create more. This is called stewardship. Discuss how you feel about making financial profit in the church. What precautions can you make so that money is earned in a godly manner and used for godly purposes?

3. Which of the assets identified above has the greatest potential to create both cash flow and missional impact?

4. Who needs to be on the team (or recruited) to get started?

CHAPTER 4
Incubating New Businesses

When cash is more available (fluid) and the church has open networks in the community, then they can incubate new businesses (position B in Figure 2.2, top right). This requires some up-front financing, but it can produce a cash flow in a short matter of time. When a church has some cash available, this approach can often provide a better return on investment (ROI) than simply parking the money in a bank. In addition, the open networks provide an available customer base for the new business.

THIRD SPACES

Shadowland Community Church (SCC) in Nicholasville, KY purchased a coffee shop in the center of the city. The goal was to provide a third space for the community during the work week as well as provide a church venue for Sundays.[24] This provided a venue to incubate several businesses. Of course, the coffee shop business provided a rental income stream to the church.[25] In addition, one of the church members opened a counseling center, which provided rent to the church (on Sunday, this counseling room is used for childcare). In addition, the church rents out the upstairs as an event space throughout the week. This event space became very popular as it served over fifty different groups in the first year. Some of these groups pay rent (wedding rehearsal dinners, birthday parties, photo shoots) while others were not charged. Once again, this provided not only a financial stream but also helped the church to engage missionally in the community. For example, SCC has opened the space for some funeral wakes of high school students as well as opened the space for the nearby high school students to study during their final exams (the church has provided free pancakes for students as they study). On Sundays, the event space is used for Sunday School.

GET CREATIVE

SCC is not unique in this approach, however. Many churches have adopted a similar creative strategy. For example, a church plant in Kansas City, MO rented out their building as a wedding space for $3,000 a night. The pastor informed me that this is booked both Friday and Saturday for most weekends in the year. In addition, the church provided space for an event planner and a photographer to incubate their businesses inside the church building. The equipment is put away and the rooms are then used for Sunday School by the church on Sundays.[26]

Several churches are getting creative with the use of their space to incubate businesses. Mark DeYmaz and Harry Li's church in Little Rock, AR opened a part of their building to a workout facility that is now heavily used during the week. Since this facility generates income that is not directly related to the mission of the church, the workout business pays the income tax liability based on the percentage of the building that they use.[27] This business, though, provides a significant portion of the church budget.[28]

NOT JUST FOR THE WEALTHY

This approach is not simply for wealthy neighborhoods. Bible Center Church in Pittsburgh, PA is in a neighborhood that has long been plagued by poverty and crime. Pastor John Wallace's passion for black-owned businesses has resulted in the church incubating a variety of businesses through their Oasis Project. This initiative spawned a transportation company, café, farm, fishery, business development center, property maintenance and management company, and an entrepreneurship academy. Several entrepreneurs to be helped this year include a chef, jewelry maker, web designer and event planner. Pastor Wallace (2019) explains that this approach is driven by missional vision, "I believe that the proliferation of small [business], even microbusiness, ownership can have a tremendously powerful impact, not only economically, but also psychologically, on communities like

Homewood." Ultimately, this strengthens the financial position of the community and church.

"BIZNISTRY"

Jeff Greer and Chuck Proudfit (2013, p. 18) in Cincinnati, OH are taking similar steps by establishing what they call biznistry, meaning a "faith-based business that generates profits for ministry," at the Grace Chapel. The Grace Chapel campus, a former manufacturing plant, provides new business incubation, acceleration, funding, training, and team building to launch several biznistries. They now have over two-dozen biznistries connected to the Grace Chapel campus, which have generated over 100 jobs, bringing thousands of people to Grace Chapel's campus each week, and are releasing about $200,000 in profits annually for ministry reinvestment (20% of the annual operating costs of the church).[29] The motivation for each of these biznistries is "to create purpose-filled, meaningful work in the business world that advances the kingdom of God" (Greer and Proudfit, 2013, p. 52). Grace Chapel, then, experiences both financial viability and missional vitality through this approach.

PRACTICE

It turns out that there is no special set of personality traits required to incubate a business. Researchers have "discovered that there are patterns in how entrepreneurs think. This means that all of us have the ability to act and think entrepreneurially with practice."[30] I liken the process of incubating a business to learning how to sail a sailboat.[31]

When living in South Dakota, the winds swept across the plains and provided a great environment for sailing. At a summer camp, I first felt the wind at my back on a Hobie catamaran sailboat and was hooked. I relished the time on the boat to learn the skills to gauge the wind, hoist the sail, manage the rudder, and fly a hull (when one of the two hulls is out of the water). I eventually purchased my own Hobie 16 catamaran sailboat and would teach others the thrill of catching the wind in their hands and being swept across the water. Figure 4.1 (page 40) shows the necessary parts of the sailboat to provide a good sailing experience, which also correspond to incubating a new business.

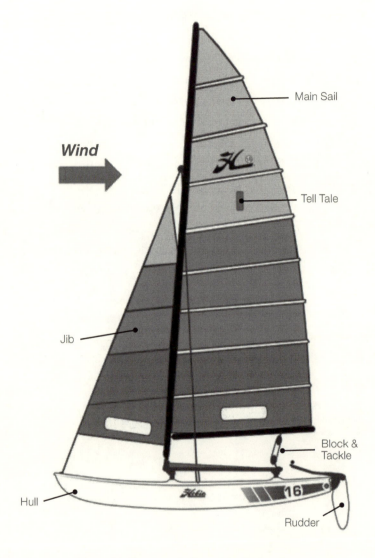

Figure 4.1: Comparing Sailing to New Business Startup

1. **Wind:** The first element of sailing is to gauge the wind (both the velocity and direction). If there is no wind, then there is no sailing. To incubate a business, this is like gauging the market demand for a particular product or service. Ask:

   - What are people looking for or requesting?
   - What problems can we solve for others?
   - How can we love and serve others?
   - How many people will we be able to serve? Business experts claim that you need to have at least twenty paying customers up front before starting.
   - Who are these people and where do they live, shop, play, etc.?

2. **Main Sail:** The main sail will simply catch the wind– that is it! For your business, you need to take the idea from above and turn it into a good product or service that "catches" the market demand. Ask:

   - How can we turn this unmet need into a product or service?
   - What skills, specializations, or knowledge do we have (or need to learn) to deliver this well?
   - What is the least costly way to set up our sail to test out the market demand?

3. **Sailing Team:** It takes more than one person to really move the boat at top speed. Ask:

   - Who else has skills, resources, experience, etc. that can help this business get started?
   - What roles are crucial and who can fill these roles?
   - Where can I find other specialists to fit niche roles?

4. **Rudder:** The rudder simply puts you in the proper position to catch the wind. You can be in the middle of vigorous wind but 'stuck in irons' going nowhere if the rudder is not positioned correctly. This is similar to positioning your product or service. Ask:

   - Where can we let people know about this product/service so that they can try it out?
   - How do we inform them using social media and other advertising?
   - Who can provide a raving review for us that is also influential with other people that they can tell?

5. **Block & Tackle:** These pulleys simply allow you to manage the sail to match the wind strength. Accordingly, businesses will need to attend to particular logistics to keep catching the market winds. Ask:

   - What specific logistics are needed for this business to be sustainable (e.g., accounting, finance, operational management, sales, marketing)?
   - Who is available and experienced to help us?

6. **Hull:** This is the part of the boat that floats on the water. You want it to be as light as possible so that it doesn't take a lot of wind to move it. For a business, this is similar to overhead. Ask:

    - What is the minimum overhead to get started? E.g., what is the minimum equipment/space needed to get started?
    - How can we minimize costs like transportation, electricity, rent, water, HVAC, etc.? E.g., can we operate in our garage instead of in a rented building?

7. **Tell Tale**: Little ribbons on the main sail inform you if the sail is catching the wind properly so that you can adjust quickly (trim the sail). This is like metrics or measures of success for a business. Ask:

    - What key metrics will we use to measure our success? Contrary to popular opinion, you cannot simply measure how many people you are serving since you can be serving lots of people but losing money on each one.
    - For Christian business, how can you measure the social and spiritual capital, in addition to the financial capital to measure success?

8. **Jib:** The main sale can work in tandem with a smaller sail in the front called a jib. The jib helps in turning the boat. In addition, another large front sail can be

hoisted, called a spinnaker, which allows you to catch more wind during times of good wind. This is similar to tandem businesses. Ask:

- Are there tandem businesses that we can also serve alongside or together? E.g., can you serve donuts or sweet cakes alongside an existing coffee shop?
- How will our business enhance or create more customers for tandem businesses? E.g., as you draw customers to your event space, can you also offer photography, event planning, Airbnb lodging, etc.?

9. **Righting Rope:** The righting rope is there in case of emergencies. If the boat gets turned over, then you can use the rope to flip it upright again. For most instances, this is not a big problem if you have planned ahead (and brought the rope). Similarly, every business should have an exit strategy. Just in case things do not go as planned and your partners want to get out, plan for how they can leave the business smoothly and with as little pain (and cost) as possible.

Once you learn the above elements, the best way to learn sailing is to go out for a short sailing excursion. Likewise, you should 'test the water' with some small business experiments before going too big. See chapter seven for more guidance in forming a Minimum Viable Product (MVP) that will serve as an initial prototype for your business. Also, see appendix A for a business model canvas to sketch out the main considerations for your business when you are ready to scale it. Just like sailing, you will learn from your initial successes and failures to develop healthy business and ministry habits. Personally, I have learned from each of the five businesses I have started – often, I learned more from the painful mistakes. Coaching (with an experienced coach)[32] can help guide you as you start learning this new skill. Once you learn the process, though, you continually improve by practice, as you trim your sail and catch the wind!

CHAPTER 5

Non-Profits Form Mission Arms of the Church

Many churches find themselves in a position whereby cash is limited, and their relational networks are shrinking or closed (position C in Figure 2.2, bottom left). While this situation appears bleak, there is hope for this church to become missionally vibrant and financially viable again. I will discuss two approaches when you are in this position. The first one is to consider forming a non-profit entity to address the issues/concerns of your community. This becomes a missional arm of your church/church plant that can receive cash flow.

NEGATIVE CASH FLOW TO POSITIVE

How would your church board respond if someone said that the church can increase their mission impact to over half a million dollars without asking for more tithes and offerings? This is what Mosaic church in Little Rock, AR accomplished through the formation of their non-profit arm called "Vine and Village." Since this non-profit is separate from the church, Vine and Village can attract government grants and donations from other entities that would not give to the church. Even other churches are donating to this non-profit due to their missional impact.[33] This separate non-profit then becomes a mission[34] arm of the church as they tackle issues such as: assisting immigration, training teen moms, offering fresh produce to 'food deserts,' providing extended family for those with disabilities, in addition to offering a chess club, clothes closet, employment training, etc.[35]

Usually, the mission budget of a church/church plant, is a negative cash draw. In other words, part of the budget of the church is to provide for ministering to the holistic needs of the community. If a non-profit is formed that is autonomous from the church, then this is no longer a negative cash draw from the church. Instead, the separate entity can seek funds from various sources that the church would not be eligible for. To maintain the missional focus of the non-profit, the church has continual representation on the non-profit's board.

CHURCH ADVANTAGES

Joy Skjegstad has worked with over 50 churches to assist in the formation of non-profits. She currently directs the Park Avenue Foundation, which is a non-profit connected to Park Avenue United Methodist Church in South Minneapolis. Skjegstad (2002) notes that "Setting up a non-profit at your church can bring together the very best aspects of the church with the outside resources that a non-profit can draw" (p. 3). She further explains how churches have several advantages for starting non-profits, such as:

1. Churches often have the trust of the community so that the church can draw participants that may not otherwise feel safe at other locations.
2. Churches have a "captive audience" among the church members, which form a volunteer pool to make the non-profit function well. This can mobilize the talents within the church to provide substantial services to the community. Skjegstad (2002) explains from her own experience at Park Avenue UMC, "Volunteer tutors, mentors, lawyers, doctors, and nurses were all mobilized from within the congregation to do good works every day of the week in the church building" (p. 3).
3. Since a church itself is considered a non-profit entity by the IRS, the church often understands the necessary structure and paperwork for a non-profit to run.

Several churches in the past have operated schools and day cares as non-profit entities. The non-profit can then pay rent to the church based on the market price (or less). This allows the church to receive an income stream once again as well as missionally impact the community through the social services provided by the non-profit. A pastor in a small community in Kentucky recently informed me his church would have closed a long time ago if it were not for the preschool in the church providing both an income stream and new relationships. Once again, both missional impact and financial viability can be achieved through this approach.

PRACTICE

Discuss with your leadership team

1. What are some of the major issues or concerns for people in your community?
2. Which of these issues or concerns is your team most passionate about seeing God transform?
3. Who else is concerned about these issues? When you have the mentality that you are cooperating with God in revealing God's kingdom on earth, you can identify potential stake holders by asking, "Who is concerned about the flourishing of this community?" You do not have to agree with these people or institutions on every point in order to work with them. In fact, they do not have to even be Christian organizations to cooperate with them. Several churches have found willing and available stakeholders in schools, local governments, police/fire departments, agricultural extension offices, other non-profits, etc.
4. Initiate conversations with the stakeholders that are concerned about the issues/concerns you have identified above. Then, look for grants from organizations that are also concerned.
5. Write the grants for the issues/concerns that your team is most concerned about. You often must write several grants in order to obtain a few. For additional help, you can hire a grant writer.

CHAPTER 6

Co-Vocational Pastoring Opens Multiple Income Streams

Another approach for churches that are both cash challenged along with closed/shrinking networks (position D in Figure 2.2, bottom left) is to consider co-vocational pastoring. Previously, the term bi-vocational was used to describe a pastor who worked a secular job outside the church. The implication was that this was not the pastor's vocational preference, and this was simply temporary until the church could afford a full salary. Once the church could afford a full salary, however, then the pastor would leave their secular job and work full-time for the church.

CO-VO VS. BI-VO

The term 'co-vocational' challenges these assumptions. Instead of regarding this as a secular job, what if the job is considered to have sacred value that provides value for others? In addition, what if this is not simply a 'second best' temporary job? Co-vocational pastors choose to continue to work outside the church even when the church can afford a full salary.[36] In this way, the church can be more generous to serve the community as well as create relational networks through the pastor's job (Brisco, 2018). In short, the job outside the church is considered sacred, the pastor's choice, and long-term versus secular, not of their choosing, and short-term.

Shadowland Community Church is a co-vocational church plant. I am one of four teaching pastors that share the preaching but only one is paid part-time for mission mobilization. The church has a goal to give away 51% of the tithes and offerings to impact the community to reveal the kingdom of God. This is unheard of for most churches since the personnel and building costs absorb much of the budget. Even for a healthy church, the personnel and buildings can require 70% of the church budget (see the Doctor's Checkup in chapter one).

NEW NORMAL

After discussing alternative church financial models with a Bishop for the Church of God In Christ (COGIC), this Bishop revealed this co-vocational approach is used by almost all of their churches. This is due to both financial and missional reasons. This was not a new practice; instead, the Bishop assumed this was (and would continue to be) the normal practice for COGIC pastors within this denomination that has grown to be the fifth largest in the U.S.[37]

Pastor Johnson Asare in Ghana, West Africa, said, "In the garden of Eden, God provided multiple streams. Perhaps, this is to ensure that there was water even if one stream dried up. Pastors also need more than one income stream because you never know which one will dry up."[38] Pastor Asare is a co-vocational pastor who has started businesses such as a hotel, shea butter processing station, cashew farm, etc. He states that he does not need money from outside of Ghana to do church planting and ministry in Ghana. Located in a Muslim majority city, he explains that the money for Christian ministry comes from Muslims who patronize his businesses!

Karl Vaters (2017), in *Christianity Today*, recently called bi-vocational ministry the "new normal" since it has increased 32% from 2010 to 2015.[39] There is a growing number of pastors that are adopting this approach for both financial and missional reasons. On the financial side, this income source helps to ease some of the major tensions in the pastor/church planters' family, particularly if the outside job provides benefits, such as health care for the family. In addition, this income source may be steadier and more reliable to provide a stable base income for planning purposes. This is particularly important in high-cost areas.

OPEN NETWORKS

Since the marketplace is a relational network whereby people exchange value, the co-vocational approach is particularly helpful to open relational networks in addition to providing another source of income. Several bi-vocational pastors/church planters end up becoming co-vocational for this very reason—it provides an open network of relationships to live out the Great Commission. In addition, a job outside the church can provide 'street cred' for those both inside and outside the church. For those outside the church, I have noticed that they view me differently if I start off the conversation as a pastor or seminary professor than if I start the conversation as an engineer or Airbnb host. For those inside the church, they also recognize that you understand their world in the marketplace; therefore, they can feel that you are more empathetic to their daily lives.

PRACTICE

1. What gifts, talents, abilities does the pastor/church planter have that can be leveraged into a job outside the church? This includes starting their own business as well as working for someone else. Of course, the business owner has more flexibility than those who work for others. Jobs that are particularly service related are ideally suited for co-vocational pastoring.
2. Can the pastor/church planter do this job with excellence? E.g., can they demonstrate their faith commitment through their honesty, compassion, generosity, and encouragement. I have noticed that these interpersonal traits stick out in many business settings such that people take notice.
3. Is there a leadership team that the co-vocational pastor can work alongside? I have experienced the benefit of working with such a team (four people) as a co-vocational pastor myself. This team can share the load of preaching, visiting, counseling, etc. such that the co-vocational pastor does not get burned out by doing all the church work *and* another outside job. This also allows for continuity of ministry when the co-vocational pastor has more stressful and demanding times at the outside job.

CHAPTER 7

Entrepreneurial Churches Locate Church Inside the Marketplace

If cash in the church is more available (fluid) and the church has closed networks (position E in Figure 2.2, bottom right), then consider an entrepreneurial church. I define Entrepreneurial Churches (EC) as,

> Entrepreneurial approaches to form communities of Christ followers among unchurched people through businesses in the marketplace. Entrepreneurial Church Plants address the need to engage public society through the marketplace via entrepreneurial means. Such entrepreneurial church planters either start new businesses or work within existing businesses to plant churches in business venues. (Moon & Long, 2018, p. 6)

ACCESS TO UNCHURCHED PEOPLE

Paul Unsworth in London, England noticed that 20,000 people a day walked down his street each weekend, yet there was no vital Christian witness.[40] Only 5% of the British attend church on a regular basis (Brierly Consultancy, 2019). How could he gain access to this large group of people and lead them to Jesus? His response was to open the Kahaila coffee shop that serves excellent coffee and cake. Unsworth explains his rationale,

> We need to find out how to form community. This is why we chose a coffee shop. It is a third space where people share life. We aim to build community in the café.
>
> For evangelism, if you like doing something, do it with others. Invite others to do it with you. You build community and listen to others.[41]

This has resulted in a church plant that also meets in the same building on Wednesday nights. He is motivated by a missional impulse to connect with the unchurched or dechurched – and it is working! Unsworth shared,

> I have had more spiritual conversations with people in a week than I had in working in a church for a whole year…[with] people that don't know anything about Jesus. We need to create opportunities to genuinely listen to people. In time, they will be interested in what I believe.

> Church is more than a service on a Sunday. Church is a spiritual family that comes together to redeem the lost.[42]

EXISTING BUSINESSES

Unsworth is not unique in this approach (Moon & Long, 2018). Instead of starting a new business, Sean Mikschl works as a waiter in an existing restaurant. This provides an open network for his church plant that meets on Thursdays at 11 PM (yes, that is in the evening) since they get off work at that time and are ready to meet. Whereas this group of employees resisted Mikschl's attempts for a church to meet at his own house, they were very open to meeting at a pub on Thursday evenings. This has led to some of the waiters coming to faith. Several venues have been used successfully to start ECs such as workout facilities, bakeries, barber shops, hotels, cafes, in addition to numerous coffee shops.[43] There are even networks being developed to encourage the opening of 'micro-churches' in the marketplace.[44]

YOUR WORK MATTERS TO GOD

In traditional church planting discussions, businessmen and women were typically not considered essential except to finance and support the mission. The unspoken message was that the real value of their business work was to use their profits to support the "spiritual work." While I applaud the generous use of profits from excellent work, my hope is that business people now find that they have a front seat at the church planting table. In short, your work matters to God![45] Even further, you will likely find the opportunity to live out your missional calling *within* the marketplace, not *in spite* of the marketplace.

When Jesus discussed the cost of being a disciple, he said,

> Suppose one of you wants to build a tower. Won't you first sit down and estimate the cost to see if you have enough money to complete it? For if you lay the foundation and are not able to finish it, everyone who sees it will ridicule you, saying, 'This person began to build and wasn't able to finish.' (Luke 14:28-31)

KEY INGREDIENTS

In order to 'count the cost' from a business perspective, Sam Altman, a venture capitalist and entrepreneur from Stanford who funded 720 businesses, recommends that entrepreneurs consider four key ingredients:

1. Good idea (that solves a need and people will pay for),
2. Good product/service (something users love and will tell others about),
3. Good team (that are smart, get things done, and work together well), and
4. Good execution (deliver with excellence in the right metrics and milestones).[46]

Understanding and applying these key ingredients will help EC planters to wisely 'build the tower.' Here are the foundational steps for ECs within the framework of entrepreneurship as described by Altman, using the acronym ABIDES:

1. **A**sk the Lord for discernment and direction
2. **B**egin with a good idea
3. **I**ncubate a good product or service
4. **D**evelop a good team
5. **E**xcel at good execution
6. **S**ustain by introducing metrics

The acronym ABIDES reminds us that our EC efforts depend integrally on abiding as branches in the Vine of the Lord who nourishes us (John 15). This approach will draw upon the Fresh Expressions[47] process to lay a missiological foundation. Then, we will integrate this with the Business Model Canvas (to be discussed shortly) to plan out the business approach for the EC plant. Lastly, we will implement the EC plant using the Lean Startup approach with pivots in a quick feedback loop (also to be discussed shortly). Since this approach is likely the most complicated of the approaches described so far, I am providing more details on this model than the others.

ASK THE LORD FOR DISCERNMENT AND DIRECTION

Prayer is often the starting point for great endeavors. Jesus himself, when burdened with compassion for the lost people around him, asked his disciples to pray that the Lord of the Harvest would send out workers for the harvest (Matthew 9:36–38). Then in the next verse at 10:1, Jesus prepared his disciples for ministry and sent them out. This pattern of observation, burden, prayer, and action appears to be a model of God prompting people for ministry. The Apostle Paul at Athens was moved in his spirit when seeing the idolatry and lostness around him. He must have been in constant prayer; and then he acted by witnessing in the synagogue and "in the marketplace day by day with those who happened to be there" (Acts 17:17). Something similar is seen in the Apostle Paul's epistles that usually begin with thanksgiving and/or prayer; often these prayers contain seminal ideas that Paul develops in the rest of the letter (e.g., 1 Corinthians 1:4–9; 1 Thessalonians 3:11–13). It is almost as if Paul's constant praying prepared him to write the letter about the very themes he was praying about. This process of EC likewise involves the preparation of prayer for purposeful, missional action. This prayer will be prompted in conjunction with careful observation of people and their needs (see below) and will involve both active expression of longing and listening to the Lord. One should pay attention to the Spirit's prompting and the yearnings that spring up in one's heart. Then, be prepared to move in mission.

BEGIN WITH A GOOD IDEA

Altman affirms, "The best ideas are mission-oriented.... There is no way to get through the pain of a startup unless you believe that the startup really matters."[48] The Fresh Expression approach provides a helpful starting point for the business idea that is mission-oriented. The first step in Fresh Expressions is listening to the community, as illustrated in Figure 7.1 below.[49]

Underpinned by prayer, ongoing listening and relationship with the wider church

Figure 7.1 Fresh Expressions Process

Listening often requires taking the time to engage people through ethnographic research methods. Participant-observation is a research method that allows the potential church planter to participate with the people long enough and deeply enough that the people express their true needs, desires, aspirations, and dreams. In addition to the needs, look for the assets that reside in this community. This indicates their strengths that can be built upon as well as their pains that need to be addressed.

Recording these participant-observations gives you research data during the listening process.

Researchers often learn from locals to give them deeper insight. The most helpful locals tend to be those who:

- Know their context well (i.e., they are 'regulars' vs. newcomers),
- Are currently involved in the context,
- Are sociable and verbal,
- Have time for you,
- Are located nearby, and
- Are not overly analytical (they just tell you what they know).

Informal interviews with locals involve a series of friendly conversations into which the interviewer slowly introduces new elements to assist the one being interviewed. In practice, this is really relationship building instead of simply interviewing. After a while, these locals may be grouped together with others into a focus group. A small focus group (six to twelve people) can represent the larger context and provide helpful responses to questions that you formulate based on the initial participant-observations. Gradually, this research should lead to a good idea for a business that expresses love through service.

INCUBATE A GOOD PRODUCT OR SERVICE

The next logical step in the Fresh Expressions approach is to find opportunities to love and serve the people that you have been listening to. As you start to love and serve in small ways, then God may present larger opportunities. This will result in a good product or service that will serve as the basis for your business. Keep in mind that this must be based on a missional foundation. It should be a calling from God and not simply a profit-making venture. Often, EC planters have found good traction in the service businesses since that provides daily conversations with larger networks of people. Once you have discovered a good idea to form a good product/service that you feel expresses your love for God and others, the next step is to organize this into a business model.

Alexander Osterwalder and Yves Pigneur explain, "A business model describes the rationale of how an organization creates, delivers, and captures value."[50] They developed an approach called the Business Model Canvas to provide "a practical guide for visionaries, game changers, and challengers eager to design or reinvent business models."[51] There are nine elements to this approach that serve as the building blocks for developing a business model. The nine elements are mapped out on paper to demonstrate the logical connections between them.[52] Sites such as www.strategyzer.com provide explanations of the nine elements as well as downloads to start the process of mapping out your business model with your church planting team.[53] The nine elements are as follows:

1. Value proposition: What needs can I solve for customers? This is what you developed from your research based upon the first two steps in the Fresh Expressions approach above.
2. Customer segments: Who will pay to solve this need and where are they located? Why would they buy this?
3. Channels: How do you distribute the products or provide the service to customers?
4. Customer Relationships: How do I get, keep, and grow customers? From a missional perspective, you are asking, "How can I continue to demonstrate love for others through serving them well?"
5. Revenue Streams: How does your business make money from each customer segment?
6. Key resources: What assets do you need to make this company work? Think of physical equipment, human resources, software, social networks, spiritual trust, etc.
7. Partners: Who are the key partners and suppliers, and what do you need them to perform and when?
8. Key Activities: What are most important activities that you need to perform to make this business work?
9. Cost Structure: What are the costs and expenses to deliver this product or service? Consider fixed and

variable costs, your breakeven point, and the Return on Investment.

These nine items do not ensure a viable and mission-focused business, but they do provide critical areas to consider keeping on track. As you begin to map out the Business Model Canvas, you will quickly realize that you do not have all of the skills or capacity for each of the items needed. That is why it is critical to develop a good team of people who have the necessary skills and gifts.

DEVELOP A GOOD TEAM

I have not met an EC planter yet who did not admit their need for a team of skilled people to come alongside of them. You will need people skilled in accounting, finance, organizational planning, taxes, etc. If you do not recruit a team with these skills, then you will quickly find yourself over your head and on a quick road to burnout. This is a great opportunity to approach people in the church that have these skills and gifts so that you can invite them into the missional opportunity of EC. Perhaps for the first time, these business people will be validated that they are essential to the *missio Dei*.

In addition to the business skills above, the EC planter will need to build a team that knows how to evangelize in word, deed, and lifestyle. While evangelism has become more complex in the 21st century than at the beginning of the 20th century, there are new opportunities for evangelism that did not exist in a previous generation as well. Dealing with issues like secularism, pluralism, individualism, relativism, identity-shifting, and technology are critical considerations for EC planters. Each of these complexities also provide opportunities for evangelism.[54]

EXCEL AT GOOD EXECUTION

Eric Ries observed that entrepreneurs often have three limitations that prevent them from initiating and executing their business.[55] As shown in Figure 7.2 (page 72),[56] the three obstacles are:

1. Incomplete Business Plans: Few EC planters are experienced with articulating business plans that address the concerns that venture capitalists are looking for. Resources are available to assist in developing business plans, but this can still be a daunting task.[57]
2. Untested Market Demands: One of the biggest uncertainties about your proposed business is, "Will people buy this good or service?" Since you have not fully tried out your business yet, you do not have an adequate answer.
3. Inadequate funding: To launch a full business with all the services that you would like to offer would require a lot of funding. Church plants are the same. Finding this amount of money is not easy, particularly when you consider that there is no guarantee the church plant will survive after burning

through the initial amount of startup money raised for the first three years.

To overcome these obstacles, Ries recommends that you do not launch your business with all the services and products exactly the way that you like. Instead, provide the minimum viable product (MVP) that would allow you to demonstrate what your business is offering. This means that you invest a small amount to get a product or service that people can experience. The initial value is *not* the amount of profit that you make; rather, Ries recommends that your initial goal is to measure your customers' reactions. In other words, allow customers to experience your business and then they provide feedback to tell you what they would prefer. The customer reaction then gives you valuable information to help you innovate and revise your business. At the same time, you are building a core group of customers that are teaching you what they want, and they appreciate your responsiveness to adapt to their needs. This develops a loyal base of customers and forms a community. This is like the third step in the Fresh Expressions approach about "building community." The last part of the feedback loop is to take this information from customers and revise/refine your MVP. Then, send it back through the feedback look again.

This level of execution requires attentiveness and a quick response to customers' needs and concerns. You will likely realize that your service to these customers may be the very way that God has provided for you to fulfill the Great Commandment. I.e., your business is now demonstrating love to others by meeting their needs better and demonstrating your love for God by using your God-given gifts and abilities to serve others with excellence.[58]

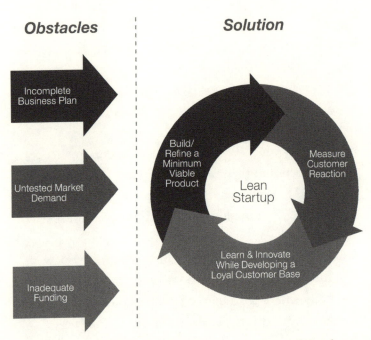

Figure 7.2 Startup Obstacles and Response with Lean Startup Approach

SUSTAIN BY INTRODUCING METRICS

A well-known maxim is, "What gets measured, gets done." In other words, the metrics that you pay attention to will affect how you direct your energies.[59] For all businesses, they must look at financial metrics. If there is no profit, then the business will eventually close, and it will not provide a service to anyone. John Wesley wisely encouraged Christian business owners to make as much profit as they can and save (not waste profit) as much as they can so that they can give as much as they can. While these are necessary conditions for business, they are not sufficient, though, for an EC. In addition, EC planters must also gauge their success via two other metrics: social capital and spiritual capital.

Social capital can be measured in various ways. The point is that this should be reported just as regularly as the financial capital numbers are reported. For example, EC planters can measure:

1. Stories of lives that are being transformed,
2. Relational networks that the EC plant is connecting with (cf. Paul and the guilds),
3. How the health and welfare (physically and emotionally) of the workers and community are affected positively by the business.

In addition to social capital, EC planters should be measuring and reporting spiritual capital. Church planters often measure this by quantitative data like the number of conversions, baptisms, small groups, etc. In addition to quantitative measures, EC planters can provide qualitative data that you cannot count with numbers alone, such as:

1. How the business has been generous in the community (cf. John Wesley's encouragement to give all that you can);
2. Signs of the Kingdom inside and around the EC plant;
3. Spiritual conversations that are started with the unchurched or de-churched;
4. Outward evidences of inward change, such as asking more and better questions about Jesus, baptism, prayer, etc.; and
5. Measures of accountability being used by the business team.

Paying attention to these metrics keeps the focus on exploring discipleship instead of simply building a business that is focused on profit alone.

PRACTICE

Gather your church/church plant team to discuss the following:

1. Start the process of brainstorming the idea, service/produce, team, and execution.
2. Begin the process of ABIDES––Ask, Begin, Incubate, Develop, Excel, Sustain.
3. As the team begins to love and serve others, look for areas that gain the most traction in the community by the creation of spiritual, social, and financial capital.
4. Collect data that will inform the business model.
5. Print Appendix A. Beginning at the center of the diagram (Value Proposition), fill in the blocks of information for each of the nine considerations for your business model.
6. Execute your minimum viable product (MVP) that allows you to demonstrate what your business is offering. Then, adjust based on the feedback received.
7. Select metrics that measure spiritual, social, and financial capital.

CHAPTER 8
Decentralized Churches

After presenting the above five financial options recently, a pastor came up to me afterwards and said, "In my situation, I do not know where to start since I am not even on your chart! My cash is so limited, and my networks are so minimal that I do not even fit into any of these options. What can I do?"

MINCED

Fortunately, there is another option for church planters and struggling churches. This can be described as Decentralized Churches. I will then update the acronym MINCE to add the sixth option (starting with the letter D) so that the acronym now is MINCED. Decentralized churches go under several names, such as house church, simple church, organic church, dinner church, fellowship band, micro-church, etc.[60] What they all have in common, though, is the gathering of small groups of Christ followers in everyday settings. The venues vary, as well as the number of people and the meeting frequency. They all challenge the existing financial models as they subtly ask the question, "When did the Sunday gathering church attendance number become the gold standard for church health? Who said that bigger is always better?" As a result, this eliminates (or greatly reduces) the largest line items for most church budgets – building mortgage/rent and salaries.

Similar to the other MINCE financial options, this model is based upon missional vibrancy as well as financial viability. E.g., the Inspire movement in both Europe and the U.S. focuses on missional engagement and discipleship as a starting point for gathering a community of Christ followers. The Tampa Underground network of churches includes house churches that focus on mission among the poor, homeless, recovering men and women, single mothers, and many more.[61]

THRIVE AMIDST PANDEMICS

The recent COVID 19 pandemic revealed the strength of Decentralized churches. In a short time, large church gatherings were prohibited. As a result, many churches gradually adapted to technology such as Zoom to maintain their connections with their congregations. Hugh Halter (2020) explains how decentralized churches actually thrived amidst the pandemic,

> Are all churches struggling? No, in fact if we understand and believe the reports that half the

> American church has already been decentralized into house churches then only half the church is struggling. "Where is the missional movement?" so many have asked the last five years? Well, the real answer is that the missional church, with decentralized form, is alive and well. Like cockroaches to the coronavirus, we know how to navigate and even prosper among the rubble. We already know how to live off the meager scraps. We are everywhere and we're healthier now than ever before.[62]

One of the surprises of the Coronavirus has been that churches have been 'forced' to decentralize for their own survival. That should bring back memories from biblical and historic times when the church survived and thrived amidst great struggle and persecution. The bigger surprise is that some churches are now asking the question if they want to return to the centralized 'church as normal' once the social isolation bans are lifted.

PRACTICE:

1. Discuss the decentralized church idea with friends/family that are willing to meet and grow in their faith. Sometimes, the impetus is a particular social concern or need that people want to address in a godly manner. Other times, people are unchurched or de-churched because they are put off by the formal church.

2. Choose a gathering venue. This could be in the home, third space, business, etc. Some church planters have noted that lower income class folks do not often prefer to meet in homes, unlike suburbanites who are happy to share their large homes and "show them off" a bit.
3. Share the leadership. Rotate the leadership based upon gifting. Some are gifted at teaching, while others may be gifted at hosting, serving, counseling, visiting, etc.
4. Keep the teaching reproducible by reading a biblical text and drawing out discussion based on what they heard. A good resource to use is the Serendipity Bible that provides lots of questions and group helps.

As with all the MINCED options, there are risks that need to be considered before considering one of these financial models. In the next chapter, I will discuss some of these cautions.

CHAPTER 9
Cautions to Consider

Discussions on money can be a bit delicate. On one hand, theologians like John Wesley recognized the great potential for wealth to be created and used to transform society. David Wright (2012, p. 95) notes, "Wesley's publishing enterprise was enormously successful. It made Wesley very wealthy. Some estimate he earned as much as 30,000 pounds (more than $6 million today) over his life from this highly successful entrepreneurial business." Reflecting on the missional significance of business and money in the marketplace, Wesley concluded, "It is therefore of the highest concern that all who fear God know how to employ this valuable talent [money]; that they be instructed how it may answer these glorious ends, and in the highest degree."[63]

On the other hand, Wesley recognized the dangers of riches. While money can be used for great good, it can also be used for selfish gain and harm. As a result, there are some precautions to consider as pastors and church planters apply economic wisdom.[64] I will briefly discuss a few.

SINGLE VS. TRIPLE BOTTOM LINE

Instead of relying upon a single bottom line for business (i.e., profit), Wesley was careful to warn employers not to hurt workers physically or mentally through their work. In addition, he warned against some work that was profitable but not beneficial for society to flourish. Today, we would term these social considerations. Those making business decisions must consider social and spiritual capital (in addition to financial capital) to mitigate against the excesses of the free market system. Today, this is called the Triple Bottom line to indicate that every business decision should consider the capital created or lost in these three sectors: social, spiritual, and financial capital. In short, just because a business deal *can* be done does not mean that it *should* be done. If you lose social and spiritual capital, even though you create financial capital, then it is not a good deal.[65]

ACCOUNTABILITY

Wesley was adamant that Christians should be in accountability groups. For entrepreneurs, they should ask questions like, "How much money did you make this month?" and "What did you do with it?" For Wesley, he encouraged entrepreneurship but not for selfish accumulation. His dictum, "Make all you can, save all you can, and give all you can"[66] is best understood by looking at the final goal – to have money to give to the poor. Accountability in business and spirituality is one way to guard against selfish excess. Craig Avery started 210Leaders.com in Lexington, KY for business folks to meet in groups of ten people every other week for accountability and encouragement. This has helped me personally to integrate my faith and business as well as 160 or so other business folks.[67]

GENEROSITY

Wesley felt that money should not find a resting place in your soul. Money is called currency, hinting that it should move and not become stagnant. He felt that it was not a sin to be wealthy, but it would be sinful to die wealthy. In Wesley's own example, "He kept none of this money [$6 million earned] for himself. All but the barest of necessities was reinvested in the work of the movement" (Wright, 2012, p. 95). I.e., generosity is a guard against greed and stockpiling wealth.

TAXES

When a business is operated inside a church, the church may be responsible to pay taxes, but not necessarily. The IRS does not consider the income to be taxable if the workers are volunteers, if the income is from rent for real property, if the goods sold are donated, if the business is conducted primarily for the convenience of its members, or if the business is related to the purpose of the church (a good reason to have a broadly stated church purpose statement). For example, Michael Batts, CPA advises,

> The best way for a church to avoid having a coffee shop or café treated as an unrelated business activity is to limit its activity to providing service in connection with events on the church's property. Doing so will help the church take advantage of the "convenience of members" exemption...If the church wants to have a full-service coffee shop or café open to the public for regular business hours, it should consider having the activity conducted substantially [or] entirely by volunteers to avoid unrelated business income. Alternatively, the church could rent a portion of its real property to an unrelated company to operate the coffee shop or café on the site. If the property is not debt-financed and the "rent" is not based on the net income of the tenant, real estate rental income is not unrelated business income.[68]

For churches to operate businesses that are not crucial to the mission of the church and do not fall into the various exemption categories, then the IRS requires the church to pay Unrelated Business Income Tax (UBIT), even though the church is a non-profit entity. To be very clear—simply pay the tax! The best way to do this is to require the business that is operating in the church space to pay this tax.[69]

COMMODIFICATION

In a market society, there is a temptation to put a value on everything, which can dehumanize people as simply customers or objects of exchange, thereby harming relationships. This can be particularly harmful in a church where relationships are meant to be more familial than market-based. For example, I encourage pastors to be wary of pyramid schemes in church since this can devolve into ulterior motives. Making decisions based on the triple bottom line mentioned above can also reduce the pull toward commodification.

JESUS OVERTURNED THE MONEY TABLES

Jesus drove out of the Temple those who were buying and selling (Matthew 21:12-13). Doesn't this imply that we should not mix business and worship? Actually, this is a rebuke against greedy business (particularly business that robs the poor) as well as a lack of prayer in church. The approaches described above attempt to return prayer to the marketplace as well as promote business that is done with integrity and honesty. DeYmaz and Li (2019) recommend that the church considers itself a "benevolent owner" such that the businesses operated inside the church pay a fair and even reduced rent for the use of the church space. Jesus actually commends the faithful steward who makes five talents from the five talents that were given. I wonder how many churches are simply sitting upon their talent instead of engaging the marketplace to create more. They may mistakenly use this one passage in Scripture at the temple to justify their inaction.

TEAMWORK

Several of the above approaches highlight the need for teamwork. Since pastors seldom make good bankers (Greer & Smith, 2016), it is best to gather with others who have skills in accounting, finance, marketing, strategic planning, etc. There are often people in the church who are skilled in these lines of work since that is what they do in their jobs. They are often excited to hear that their skills are needed in the church and can be put to great use for the kingdom.

CHARGING FOR BLESSINGS

In Acts 8, Simon the sorcerer tries to purchase spiritual blessing from Simon Peter and John. The harsh rebuke by the apostles should remind us that spiritual blessings are gifts from God and should not be charged. This is a stern warning for those in the Prosperity Gospel movement that attempt to create wealth by promising certain spiritual blessings.

FUNCTIONAL PLATFORMS

When businesses are simply regarded as functional platforms to get access to people, then this may lead to shoddy business practices. The Business As Mission movement in restricted access countries has been accused of this practice at times. Instead of regarding the business as simply a functional device to evangelize people, we need to be reminded that the first act of worship in the marketplace is to do our jobs with excellence. Shoddy business practice is not a credible witness of God's calling upon our lives. Dorothy Sayers says it eloquently, "No crooked legs or ill-fitted drawers ever, I dare swear, came out of the carpenter's shop at Nazareth."[70] Both the inherent worth of the value creation developed by work and the value of evangelism are important and need to both be emphasized in these financial models.[71]

CORPORATE SOCIAL RESPONSIBILITY (CSR)

Corporate Social Responsibility has become a popular trend in many businesses for various reasons. This is meant to satisfy customers that the business is actually providing a positive social benefit. While this sounds good, CSR can be used by a non-ethical business practice to justify this practice since they rationalize that they are doing much good in the end. For example, I observed a "Pay Day Loan" that was making loans with exorbitant interest rates, which often led to heavy debt among an at-risk community. They later opened a youth center in the same community to demonstrate their CSR! In Christian circles, this can take the form of trying to redeem a harmful business practice by the owners simply using the profit for additional offerings and tithes. John

Wesley encountered this problem in the eighteenth-century and developed guidelines for business practices. He noted that the workers should not be physically or mentally harmed, and there should be no harm to society.[72]

PRACTICE

1. Which of the caution areas is most resonant with your church/church plant vision?
2. What structures will you put in place so that you are not deceived by riches?
3. Who will keep you and your team accountable? Select mentors and coaches that have the best intentions for your church/church plant and will keep you honest by asking hard questions.
4. One of the best ways to prevent your team from falling to temptations of the world is to maintain intimacy with Jesus that is more attractive than the world. What spiritual practices will you maintain in order to maintain intimacy with Jesus?
5. Consider joining an accountability/encouragement group of business folks. One example of a biblically based curriculum is the 210leaders.com.

CHAPTER 10
Your Turn!

Former Anglican Bishop Graham Cray has noted, "The long-established ways of doing church are working less and less."[73] He could very easily have been referring to the changing financial picture of the church as well as missional effectiveness. The financial challenges facing the church actually offer new approaches for the church budget beyond simply tithes and offerings.

NO QUICK FIX

While there is no quick fix to the financial difficulties facing churches and church plants, considering the combination of network access (closed or open) and financial liquidity (frozen or fluid) provides useful options for both missional vibrancy and financial viability. This book is not meant to belittle tithes and offerings. On the contrary, they are essential for the church and its members. On the other hand, this book attempts to address the question, "How does the church/church plant survive when tithes and offerings are not enough to meet the church's budget to fulfill her mission?"

COMBINING FINANCIAL APPROACHES

Let's return to the church that we initially discussed in chapter one: Highland Heights Baptist Church in Memphis, TN. Instead of demolishing their 76-year-old building, they recognized that they could monetize their greatest asset: the building. Presently, the Collegiate School of Memphis operates a school in the building during the week while the church continues its services on Sunday. In addition, the nondenominational Avenue Community Church also meets in the building. These three organizations now support Heights CDC, which is a non-profit community development corporation working to improve economics, housing, green spaces, and community identity in The Heights area. While I discussed these six alternative financial models as discrete separate options, Highland Heights Baptist Church portrays how they can be combined with each other in creative ways. What has been the result?

MISSIONAL VIBRANCY AND FINANCIAL VIABILITY

Larry Reed with the Collegiate School of Memphis, noted that new life has been breathed into the church and community: "In 2006 or 2007, if you would have driven by those buildings, they were either vacant or largely unused by the church and minimally, if at all, maintained. Now they have lots of life."[74] In addition to financial stability, Christina Crutchfield (Heights CDC Community

Engagement Coordinator) explained how the church and school is also having a missional impact in the community, "Collegiate is a great partner with the neighborhood because instead of just existing . . . they actually go out into the neighborhood and do service projects."[75]

What do you do when tithes and offerings are not enough? Consider the MINCED financial options—it may make the difference between shuttering operations or bringing life back into the church. In addition, this can provide capacity to match your compassion for missional impact in your community.

As you move forward, it is crucial to consider *both* missional vibrancy and financial viability. If the two are not coupled together, then we can still miss God's intent for our church. Missiologist Leslie Newbigin once said, "A Christian community which makes its own self enlargement its primary task may be acting against God's will."[76] I.e., we are discussing financial viability not as an end in itself; rather, this is a means to increase the church's missional vibrancy.

CHALLENGE AND ENCOURAGEMENT

Human behavior often changes when there is a balance between challenge and encouragement. Whether it is learning to sail or learning a new financial model, both encouragement and challenge are needed to move forward. If there is insufficient encouragement, then people often get overwhelmed and tend to quit. On the other hand, if there is insufficient challenge, then people tend to get complacent and not change. In this book, I provide examples of each of these models that are working to encourage you that you are not alone. I hope that you learn from their examples and recognize that these alternatives are all possible.

My prayer is that the examples provided in the book stimulate new possibilities. I hope that your church or church planting team will overcome the 'curse of knowledge' and venture out in creative ways inspired by the Holy Spirit. By heeding the necessary precautions and venturing out with the model best suited to your context, the best days of your church and church plant can still be ahead.

DAILY PRAYER

In order to leave you with a final challenge, Sir Francis Bacon, adventurer, sea captain and knight in the 16th century, will have the last word. I am reminded of his prayer daily as his words hang on my office wall. Consider this challenge for your church as you encounter the folks who utter the most five deadly words, "We never did that before."

> Disturb us, Lord, when
> We are too pleased with ourselves,
> When our dreams have come true
> Because we dreamed too little,
> When we arrived safely
> Because we sailed too close to the shore.

Disturb us, Lord, when
with the abundance of things we possess
We have lost our thirst
For the waters of life;
Having fallen in love with life,
We have ceased to dream of eternity
And in our efforts to build a new earth,
We have allowed our vision
Of the new Heaven to dim.

Disturb us, Lord, to dare more boldly,
To venture on wilder seas
Where storms will show Your mastery;
Where losing sight of land,
We shall find the stars.

We ask you to push back
The horizons of our hopes;
And to push back the future
In strength, courage, hope, and love.

This we ask in the name of our Captain,
Who is Jesus Christ.[77]

PRACTICE

Gather your team for reflection and discussion. Use a big white board or large paper sheets to harvest all of the good ideas. It is often best to do the initial ideation analogue (free hand) instead of digital, so resist the temptation to use a computer to record the contributions too early.

1. Review your responses to the previous practice exercises in silence. Let each person reflect and gather their thoughts.
2. Discuss the church's health checkup as well as the financial liquidity and relational access. Where do you fit in Figure 2.2?
3. Ask your team for their best ideas for their church's financial model. Each person describes their proposal and then writes it on the board.
4. After all the ideas have been recorded, use the nominal group technique to rank the most favorable approaches.[78]
5. Set a pilot experiment that will help you to collect feedback from this initial prototype. To convince others of your proposal, a good prototype is more important than a good business plan initially.
6. Ask the question, "If we were bold people, how would God have us step out in faith?" Consider Sir Francis Drake's prayer as you deliberate.
7. It may help to establish a relationship with a coach that walks with you through the next steps. The coach's role is *not* to have all the answers; rather, their role

is to listen well and ask questions based upon what they hear and what they have experienced. There are many coaches available. You can contact the author for recommendations at: jay.moon@asburyseminary.edu. I am also an experienced coach with the Missional Formation Coaching network.[79]

8. As you consider the next steps, get in conversation with others who are implementing these financial models. If you are able, go visit them, listen to their stories, and compare your context to theirs. Try to determine:
    - How is their context similar/different to yours?
    - What successes/failures have they encountered?
    - If they were to do it all over again, what advice would they offer?
    - Practice a double listening: one ear listens to their story and the other ear listens to the Holy Spirit.

APPENDIX
Business Model Canvas

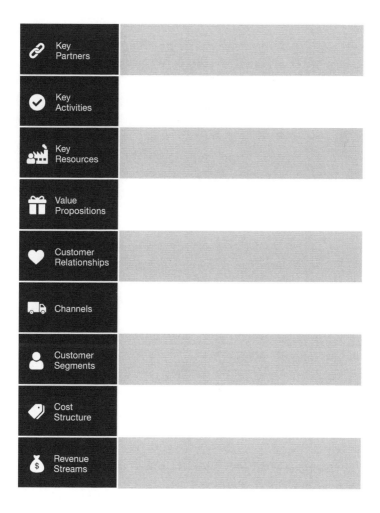

For this resource and others, see: https://www.strategyzer.com/

NOTES

1   These numbers were reported in a general email titled "Church Answers: Featuring Thom Rainer," 03/04/2021. No basis was provided for this estimate.

2   To learn more about this church's journey, see Tatum (2020).

3   I heard this figure from a presentation made by a representative of Stadia (one of the largest church planting networks in the U.S.) at the Exponential church planting conference in Orlando, FL in March, 2018. Another representative of Stadia recently informed me in April, 2021 that the figure is likely even more now.

4   Accurate numbers for church plants and closings are not easy to obtain. These estimates are from Dr. Winfield Bevins, Director of Church Planting at Asbury Theological Seminary, in conversation in 2019.

5   https://pushpay.com/blog/church-giving-statistics/

6   The rescinding of the church property tax exemption was prominent in national news again in November, 2019 when a presidential candidate said, "Yes" when asked if he thought "religious institutions like colleges, churches, and charities, should lose their tax-exempt status if they oppose same-sex marriage?" (Lybrand, H. and Subramaniam, T., 2019).

7   I whole heartedly affirm the collection of tithes and offerings. This book, though, offers creative

approaches to use the resources at the church's disposal to reveal the kingdom of God when tithes and offerings alone are not sufficient to meet the budget for various reasons.

8   Andy Crouch predicts that every organization (including church) is now in startup mode since the COVID 19 pandemic has created a new ecosystem, similar to a small 'ice age.' If churches simply try to get 'back to normal,' they will likely not survive since the ecosystem has changed so quickly. See: *https://journal.praxislabs.org/leading-beyond-the-blizzard-why-every-organization-is-now-a-startup-b7f32fb278ff*. Accessed 03/16/2021.

9   Molina-RNS, Alejandra, "Black and Latino Church Planters Hit Hard by Coronavirus Shutdown." Christianity Today, March 30, 2020. See: https://www.christianitytoday.com/news/2020/march/church-plants-new-york-latino-african-american-coronaviru.html. Accessed 03/23/2021.

10   John Wesley provides inspiration here since he was a businessman and theologian. To learn more about his approach to business and entrepreneurship, see: W. Jay Moon, Ban Cho, and Nick Bettis. "John Wesley, Compassionate Entrepreneur: A Wesleyan View of Business and Entrepreneurship," *Transformation: An International Journal of Holistic Mission Studies* 38, 2 (2021): 105–123.

11   During the RESET conference held by Exponential on May 19, 2021, Chris Lewis with Thrivent noted that he used to recommend that churches have cash

reserves for 30-60 days. Following the COVID pandemic, he now recommends that churches have 90 days of cash reserves. He also recommended that at least 50% of the giving should be online since this "became the lifeblood for churches during COVID."

12   The benchmark numbers mentioned here are from a webinar presentation on 06/04/2020 titled, "Expert Interview: Cash Flow Management, Budgeting, and Church Financial Strategies in 2020" by Stan Reiff, Partner, CapinCrouse and Joe Park, CEO, Horizon Stewardship. Both organizations have provided a wonderful service to the body of Christ by their advice and consultations.

13   The COVID pandemic has further aggravated this situation. In May 2020, CapinCrouse noted that 56% of all churches experienced a decline in overall giving. Of the churches that experienced a decline, 41% noted that this decrease was 2-10%. See Faulk, Rob, and Stan Reiff. *How Has COVID-19 Affected Your Church's Giving?* Accessed on 07/06/2021 at: https://www.capincrouse.com/wp-content/uploads/2020/04/CapinCrouse-2020-Impact-of-COVID-19-on-Church-Giving.pdf.

14   Monetize is simply the process of turning a non-revenue-generating item into cash.

15   For a healthy discussion on church economics amidst COVID-19, see the webinar on 05/02/2020 led by Mark DeYmaz titled "Church Economics: The Time to Pivot Is Now." Accesses on 07/06/2021 at: https://www.youtube.com/watch?v=hj3QC8aovXE.

16   Win and Charles Arn (1988) interviewed 17,000 people and asked, "What or who was responsible for your coming to Christ and to your church?" Following Arn's research, Gary McIntosh (2014) did a similar survey in 2000 with 1,000 participants and found some changes whereby the friend and family influence reduced to 58.9%, and 17.3% came to Jesus and church through a church staff member. Even still, the family and friend connection was by far the leading influence.

17   Hunter (2009, p. 62) considered the relational networks of new believers to be particularly crucial for church growth due to the following reasons: "(a) New disciples still have many more contacts with pre-Christian people than long-established members have. (b) They still remember what it was like to try to make sense of one's life without Jesus Christ as Lord; many longtime members have forgotten. (c) Their faces and lives still reflect the contagion of a new discovery; many friends and relatives knew them 'BC.' (d) They have not yet had time to become linguistically corrupted by theologians and preachers; they still understand and speak the language of the secular marketplace. So, for such reasons, growing churches often have a very intentional, deliberate, ongoing practice of reaching out to people in the networks of their newest members and Christians."

18   De-churched means that they formerly attended church, but they have not been a regular attender at a church for a while. The focus of this church/church planting approach is *not* to take people away from their existing church; rather, we are focusing on those who do not presently have a church home.

19   For a more detailed discussion on the Quick Ratio, see: Seth, Shobhit, "Quick Ratio" in *Investopedia*, 03/31/2021, accessed on 07/06/2021 at: https://www.investopedia.com/terms/q/quickratio.asp.

20   For purposes of a church budget, I have inserted the term "pledges" in the place of "accounts receivable." For businesses, "accounts receivable" refers to the amount of money that customers owe the company based on goods or services already received. While church members do not owe the church exactly, pledges may be a reasonable indication of the church's ability to access cash from the goodwill of the members. If this is not a reasonable assumption or if the church does not request pledges, then this value should be deleted from the equation.

21   WeWork has capitalized on this need for work space and relational connections across the U.S. (Bliss, 2018).

22   As of November 2019, Airbnb states that they have experienced a 153% compound growth rate since 2009 with 150 million total users worldwide and over half a billion Airbnb stays all-time. Millennials account for roughly 60% of all guests who have ever booked on Airbnb. $20,619 is the average expected annual profit of Airbnb hosts renting out a full two-bedroom apartment or house in major cities. For these and further statistics, see Bustamante, J. (2019).

23   Entrepreneurs may be willing to enter rental arbitrage with these types of facilities. This means that the entrepreneur will pay the church a set monthly amount for rent, then the entrepreneur will use the Airbnb or

work collective market to increase their income above the amount of the rent.

24   Actually, two churches now meet in this same space on Sunday (when the business is closed). In addition to SCC meeting on Sunday morning, a church that ministers to the recovery community meets on Sunday night.

25   At the time of this writing, the owner of the coffee shop closed her business but another business has started to provide event space. This demonstrates the flexibility and continuance of businesses in a particular space.

26   In this case, the church monetizes their underutilized asset by charging rent (the first approach) while the church or community members incubate a business (second approach). The end result puts the church and community in a stronger financial position.

27   This is called Unrelated Business Income Tax or UBIT. Churches should ask the business entity to pay this tax based on the % of the building that they are using. In this way, the church protects their non-profit status while still complying with IRS tax rules.

28   DeYmaz and Li (2019) recommend that churches find entrepreneurs in the church to start small businesses based on the existing services that the church provides. E.g., instead of the church giving away free (and poor quality) coffee, make this a coffee business that sells coffee and uses some of the profits for ministries in the church (e.g., youth group expenses). In this way, the small business benefits the church and community financially.

29   According to an email from Chuck Proudfit to the author on 12/12/19.

30   Heidi M. Neck, Christopher P. Neck, and Emma L. Murray, *Entrepreneurship: The Practice and Mindset* (Thousand Oaks, CA: Sage, 2018), 9.

31   Photo and diagram of Hobie Cats are from: https://www.hobie.com/sail/hobie-16/#. Accessed on 03/15/2021.

32   The author coaches small business owners as well as church planters. He presently has five small businesses that are all profitable, in addition to being a teaching pastor for an entrepreneurial church plant. For more information about possible coaching or coaching training, contact Jay Moon at: w@moons.com

33   To be clear, the non-profit does not feed money to the church outside of rent or typical business expenses. Instead, the non-profit simply fulfills a missional function of the church without the church paying for it.

34   Vine and Village started from the holistic work of the church as they attempted to integrate three components for community transformation, as described by their mission statement, "To be a catalyst to serve people living in and around Little Rock's emerging University District by helping to meet their social, economic and spiritual needs resulting in *Real Community Transformation*." Vine and Village, "About Us," accessed on 07/06/2021 at: https://vineandvillage.org/about-us-2/.

35   Started in 2008, this non-profit seeks to transform the community through spiritual, social, and economic means. Under the leadership of its executive director, Paul Kroger, this ministry continues to expand.

36   Send Institute commissioned a survey of bi-vocational pastors in 2018 and found that "41% indicated

that being bi-vocational was integral to a long-term ministry strategy," pointing to their preference for co-vocational ministry (Yang, 2019).

37 Philip E. Jenks, "Catholics, Mormons, Assemblies of God Growing; Mainline Churches Report a Continuing Decline," National Council of Churches, 02/12/2010. Accessed on 07/06/2021 at: http://www.ncccusa.org/news/100204yearbook2010.html.

38 Based on a personal conversation with Johnson Asare in 2014.

39 Based on a 2015 Faith Communities Today survey, fewer than two-thirds (62.2%) of U.S. churches have a full-time pastor. That's down from 71.4% in 2010. That means that bi-vocational pastoring went from 28.6% in 2010 to 37.8% in 2015. For African-American pastors, the bi-vocational rate soared to 57% (Vaters, 2017). For further trends in bi-vocational ministry, see Earls, A. (2016).

40 Based on a conversation with Paul at the Kahaila coffee shop in January, 2019.

41 Paul Unsworth, "Kahaila at #BUScot15, Part 2," Baptist Union of Scotland, 10/29/2015. Accessed on 07/06/2021 at: https://www.youtube.com/watch?v=ma-RQfrBmqk.

42 Paul Unsworth, "Kahaila - Update Jan 14," Fresh Expressions, 01/06/2014. Accessed on 07/06/2021 at: https://www.youtube.com/watch?v=eLEEh1K_W8g.

43 The Fresh Expressions director in the U.S. mentioned that over 100 such churches have been planted across the U.S. in places like coffee shops, bars, cafes,

workout facilities, pizza shops, etc. I wish there were time to mention more of these examples, such as The Table Cafe started by United Methodist Pastor Larry Foss as an approach to plant an ECP in a marginalized section of Louisville, KY. See http://www.tablecafe.org/

44 E.g., there are over 200 micro-churches in the Tampa Underground. For more information, see: https://www.tampaunderground.com/our-microchurches. In addition, Common Thread in Birmingham, AL, has incubated over fourteen businesses. For more information, see: https://commonthread.org/.

45 For a further elaboration of this from a pastoral perspective, see Tom Nelson, *Work Matters: Connecting Sunday Worship to Monday Work* (Wheaton, IL: Crossway, 2011).

46 Lecture at Stanford by Sam Altman on September 23, 2014 titled "Lecture 1 - How to Start a Startup." See: https://www.youtube.com/watch?v=CBYhVcO4WgI. Accessed 05/21/2021.

47 "Fresh Expressions is a form of church for our changing culture, established primarily for the benefit of those who are not yet part of any church." Fresh Expressions, "About," 2021. Accessed on 07/06/2021 at: https://freshexpressionsus.org/about/#what. Started in 2004 in England, this movement has spawned a network of churches that use a similar process to reach those outside the church in creative "fresh" venues.

48 Sam Altman, 09/23/2014.

49   Fresh Expressions, "Practicalities: The Fresh Expressions Journey." Accessed on 07/06/2021 at: https://freshexpressions.org.uk/find-out-more/practicalities-the-fresh-expressions-journey/.

50   Alexander Osterwalder and Yves Pigneur, *Business Model Generation: A Handbook for Visionaries, Game Changers, and Challengers* (Hoboken, NJ: John Wiley & Sons, 2010), 14.

51   Ibid, 5.

52   For a quick demonstration, see: "The Business Model Canvas - 9 Steps to Creating a Successful Business Model - Startup Tips," The Business Channel, 09/05/2015, accessed at: https://www.youtube.com/watch?v=IP0cUBWTgpY.

53   To download a copy of the business model canvas, as well as access additional resources for business startups, go to: https://strategyzer.com/canvas

54   See the following video-enhanced i-Book (on the iBook app of any Apple device) to understand and address these concerns by W. Jay Moon, Timothy Robbins, Irene Kabete, eds. *Practical Evangelism for the 21st Century: Complexities and Opportunities* (Nicholasville, KY: DOPS, 2017).

55   Eric Ries, *The Lean Startup: How Today's Entrepreneurs Use Continuous Innovation to Create Radically Successful Businesses* (New York: Crown Business, 2011).

56   This graphic was developed by the graphic software company "Smartdraw" in an email correspondence to the author in 2017.

57   Asbury Theological Seminary has developed the following resource to assist social entrepreneurs to develop their businesses, which can also assist ECP planters; see Robert A. Danielson, ed. *Social Entrepreneur: The Business of Changing the World* (Franklin, TN: Seedbed Publishing, 2015).

58   Drawing from Matthew 25 and Martin Luther, this point is made by Gene Edward Veith, Jr., *God at Work: Your Christian Vocation in All of Life* (Wheaton, IL: Crossway, 2002).

59   For further explanation about shifting church metrics to be more missional, see Reggie McNeal, *Missional Renaissance: Changing the Scorecard for the Church*, Jossey-Bass Leadership Network Series (San Francisco: Jossey Bass, 2009).

60   You could also place the multi-site option in this list, but the multi-site option has a more central hub than the others listed. I know of several financially challenged churches that have reached out to a larger church to become one of their multi-sites. This has kept the struggling church open while also allowing more lay involvement.

61   For more information, see Tampa Underground's website at https://www.tampaunderground.com/our-microchurches

62   Halter, Hugh. "Cockroaches and the Coronavirus." *Outreach,* April 7, 2020. Accessed on 07/06/2021 at: https://outreachmagazine.com/interviews/54120-cockroaches-and-the-coronavirus.html.

63 John Wesley, "The Use of Money," The Sermons of John Wesley – Sermon 50, Wesley Center Online, accessed on 07/06/2021 at: http://wesley.nnu.edu/john-wesley/the-sermons-of-john-wesley-1872-edition/sermon-50-the-use-of-money/. Wesley's sermons are available at the Wesley Center Online (n.d.). Several of his sermons dealt with topics related to money, including:
- Sermon 87 - The Danger Of Riches, 1 Tim 6:9
- Sermon 112 - The Rich Man And Lazarus, Luke 16:31
- Sermon 50 - The Use Of Money, Luke 16:9
- Sermon 51 - The Good Steward, Luke 21:2
- Sermon 108 - On Riches, Matt 19:24
- Sermon 126 - On The Danger Of Increasing Riches, Ps 62:10

64 While there is not space in this article to discuss theological underpinnings for economic wisdom, see the Economic Wisdom Project (n.d.) for helpful resources.

65 For a further discussion on the balancing of financial, social, and spiritual capital, see Danielson (2015).

66 John Wesley, "The Use of Money."

67 This group is based on scriptural principles (but not limited to Christian participation) to build yourself, build your business, and lead others. See: https://www.210leaders.com/.

68 Batts (2020).

69 For a helpful resource on UBIT from a CPA that works with several churches, see: Micahel E. Batts, *Unrelated Business Income and the Church: The Concise and Complete Guide – 2020 Edition.* (Orlando, FL: Accountability Press, 2020).

70 Dorothy Sayers, "Why Work?" In *Creed or Chaos?* (New York: Harcourt Brace, 1949): 56-57.

71 See Richard Higginson, "Mission and Entrepreneurship," *Anvil Journal of Theology and Mission* 33.1 (2017): 15–20. Higginson's recent research on kingdom businesses in the UK found that the Christian business owners identified the following means to express their kingdom impact: make the world a better place by providing an excellent product or service, embody Christian values in their workplace, share their faith in the marketplace, and giving to charitable and Christian causes.

72 Wesley Center Online (n.d.)

73 Personal conversation between the author and Graham Cray in York, England in January, 2017.

74 Tatum (2020).

75 Ibid.

76 Newbigin, Lesslie. *The Gospel in a Pluralist Society* (Grand Rapids, MI: William B. Eerdmans, 1989), 135.

77 Sir Francis Drake, "An Annual Re-post: Sir Francis Drake's Prayer (1577) 'Disturb Us, Lord,'" Maggie's Farm. 01/15/2012. Accessed on 07/06/2021 at: http://maggiesfarm.anotherdotcom.com/archives/1733-Sir-Francis-Drakes-Prayer-1577.html.

78   For a cursory description of Nominal Group Technique, see: https://en.wikipedia.org/wiki/Nominal_group_technique. Accessed 03/05/2021.

79   Several coaching networks exist to help. The MFC exists to offer training and coaching that promotes healthy rhythms and missional innovation, particularly suited for pastors and church planters. See: https://missionalformationcoaching.com/.

BIBLIOGRAPHY

NOTE: Much of the material for this book is adapted from the two publications by W. Jay Moon below.

Altman, Sam. "Lecture 1 - How to Start a Startup." Lecture at Stanford on 09/23/2014. Accessed at: https://www.youtube.com/watch?v=CBYhVcO4WgI.

Arn, Win, & Arn, Charles. *The Master's Plan for Making Disciples: Every Christian an Effective Witness Through an Enabling Church, Second ed.* Grand Rapids, MI: Baker Books, 1988.

Batts, Michael E. *Unrelated Business Income and the Church: The Concise and Complete Guide - 2020 Edition.* Orlando, FL: Accountability Press, 2020.

Bliss, Laura. How WeWork Has Perfectly Captured the Millennial Id. *The Atlantic.* February 5, 2018. Retrieved from: https://getpocket.com/explore/item/how-wework-has-perfectly-captured-the-millennial-id?utm_source=pocket-newtab.

Bradley, Jayson D. *Church Giving Statistics, 2019 Edition.* Pushpay, July 18, 2018. Retrieved from: https://pushpay.com/blog/church-giving-statistics/.

Brierley Consultancy. Christianity in the UK. Measuring the Christian population in the UK. *Faith Survey,* December 6, 2019. Retrieved from: https://faithsurvey.co.uk/uk-christianity.html.

Brisco, Brad. *Covocational Church Planting: Aligning Your Marketplace Calling and the Mission of God*. Alpharetta, GA: Send, 2018.

Bustamante, Jaleesa. Airbnb Statistics. *Property Management*, November, 2019. Retrieved from: https://ipropertymanagement.com/airbnb-statistics.

Danielson, Robbie, ed. *Social Entrepreneur: The Business of Changing the World*. Franklin, TN: Seedbed Publishing, 2015.

DeYmaz, Mark, & Li, Harry. *The Coming Revolution in Church Economics: Why Tithes and Offerings are No Longer Enough and What You Can Do About it*. Grand Rapids, MI: Baker, 2019.

Earls, Aaron. Second Shift: Thriving in Bivocational Ministry. *Lifeway*, September 29, 2016. Retrieved from: https://factsandtrends.net/2016/09/29/second-shift-thriving-in-bivocational-ministry/.

Economic Wisdom Project. *Oikonomia Network*, n.d., Retrieved from: https://oikonomianetwork.org/economic-wisdom-project/.

Grant, Adam. *Originals: How Non-Conformists Move the World*. New York: Penguin, 2016.

Greer, Jeff, & Proudfit, C. *Biznistry: Transforming Lives Through Enterprise*. Mason, OH: P5 Publications, 2013.

Greer, Peter, & Phil Smith. *Created to Flourish: How Employment-Based Solutions Help Eradicate Poverty*. Lancaster, PA: Hope, 2016.

Halter, Hugh. Cockroaches and the Coronavirus. *Outreach,* April 7, 2020. Retrieved from: https://outreachmagazine.com/interviews/54120-cockroaches-and-the-coronavirus.html.

Hunter, George G. *The Apostolic Congregation: Church Growth Reconceived for a New Generation.* Nashville, TN: Abingdon Press. Kindle Edition, 2009.

Lybrand, Holmes and Subramaniam, Tara. Fact check: O'Rourke said he would support removing tax-exemptions for religious institutions that oppose same sex marriage. Is that legal? *CNN politics,* October 11, 2019. Retrieved from: https://www.cnn.com/2019/10/11/politics/beto-orourke-lgbtq-gay-marriage-church-fact-check/index.html.

Mazareanu, Elena. Number of coworking spaces in the United States from 2007 to 2022. *Statista,* 2019. Retrieved from: https://www.statista.com/statistics/797546/number-of-coworking-spaces-us/.

McGavran, Donald. *The Bridges of God* (Second edition). Pasadena, CA: Fuller Seminary Press, 1981.

McIntosh, Gary. What Person Led You to Faith in Christ? *Good Book Blog, Talbot School of Theology,* October 29, 2014. Retrieved from: https://www.biola.edu/blogs/good-book-blog/2014/what-person-led-you-to-faith-in-christ.

Mueller, Jim. Financial Liquidity. *Investopedia*, July 14, 2019. Retrieved from: https://www.investopedia.com/articles/basics/07/liquidity.asp.

Molina-RNS, Alejandra. Black and Latino Church Planters Hit Hard by Coronavirus Shutdown. *Christianity Today*, March 30, 2020. Retrieved from: https://www.christianitytoday.com/news/2020/march/church-plants-new-york-latino-african-american-coronaviru.html.

Moon, W. Jay. "Alternative Financial Models for Churches and Church Plants: When Tithes and Offerings Are Not Enough." *Great Commission Research Journal* 12(1): 19-42. 2020.

Moon, W. Jay, & Long, F., eds. *Entrepreneurial Church Planting: Engaging Business and Mission for Marketplace Transformation*. Wilmore, KY: GlossaHouse, 2018.

Moon, W. Jay, Ban Cho, and Nick Bettis. "John Wesley, Compassionate Entrepreneur: A Wesleyan View of Business and Entrepreneurship," *Transformation: An International Journal of Holistic Mission Studies* 38, 2 (2021):105–123.

Neck, Heidi M., Christopher P. Neck, and Emma L. Murray, *Entrepreneurship: The Practice and Mindset*. Thousand Oaks, CA: Sage, 2018.

Nelson, Tom. *The Economics of Neighborly Love: Investing in Your Community's Compassion and Capacity*. Downers Grove, IL: IVP Books, 2017.

Newbigin, Lesslie. *The Gospel in a Pluralist Society*. Grand Rapids, MI: Eerdmans, 1989.

Osterwalder, Alexander and Yves Pigneur, *Business Model Generation: A Handbook for Visionaries, Game Changers, and Challengers*. Hoboken, NJ: John Wiley & Sons, 2010.

Papazov, Svetlana. *Church for Monday: Equipping Believers for Mission at Work*. FL: Living Parables, 2019.

Paul, Doug. *Kingdom Innovation: Ready or Not For a Brave New World*. 100 Movements, 2020. www.100mpublishing.com.

Ries, Eric. *The Lean Startup: How Today's Entrepreneurs Use Continuous Innovation to Create Radically Successful Businesses*. New York: Crown Business, 2011.

Skjegstad, Joy, *Starting a Nonprofit at Your Church*. Alban Institute Series. Lanham, MD: Rowman & Littlefield, 2002.

Tatum, Leigh. Faith in Action: Sharing space to save historic churches, *High Ground*, January 15, 2020. Retrieved from: https://www.highgroundnews.com/features/SavingChurchesHeights.aspx.

Tomberlin, Jim and Warren Bird. *Better Together: Making Church Mergers Work, Expanded and Updated*. Minneapolis, MN: Fortress, 2020.

Unsworth, Paul. "Kahaila - update Jan14", Fresh Expressions, 01/06/2014. Accessed on 07/06/2021 at: https://www.youtube.com/watch?v=eLEEh1K_W8g

Unsworth, Paul. "Kahaila at #BUScot15 Part 2", Baptist Union of Scotland, 10/29/2015. Accessed on 07/06/2021 at: https://www.youtube.com/watch?v=ma-RQfrBmqk

Vaters, Karl. The New Normal: 9 Realities And Trends In Bivocational Ministry, *Christianity Today,* December 12, 2017. Retrieved from: https://www.christianitytoday.com/karl-vaters/2017/december/new-normal-9-realities-trends-bivocational-ministry.html?paging=off.

Wallace, John cited by Gannon, J. Bringing Business Back to a Blighted Neighborhood, *Pittsburgh Post-Gazette*, November 4, 2019. Retrieved from: https://www.post-gazette.com/business/bop/2019/11/04/Homewood-entrepreneurship-business-pittsburgh-Bible-Center-Church/stories/201910210110.

Wesley Center Online (n.d.). Retrieved from: http://wesley.nnu.edu/john-wesley/the-sermons-of-john-wesley-1872-edition/the-sermons-of-john-wesley-theological-topic/.

Wright, David. *How God Makes the World A Better Place: A Wesleyan Primer on Faith, Work, and Economic Transformation.* Grand Rapids, MI: Christian's Library Press, 2012.

Yang, Daniel. Convergence of Vocation: A Covocational Primer for Church Planting Networks. *Send Institute,* February 5, 2019. Retrieved from: https://www.sendinstitute.org/covocational-primer/.

ABOUT THE AUTHOR

W. Jay Moon, PhD, MBA, PE served 13 years as a missionary with SIM, largely in Ghana, West Africa among the Builsa people focusing on church planting and water development, along with his wife and four children. He is presently a Professor of Evangelism & Church Planting and Director of the Office of Faith, Work, and Economics at Asbury Theological Seminary. He has authored six books, including *Intercultural Discipleship: Learning from Global Approaches to Spiritual Formation*. He also edited four books, including *Entrepreneurial Church Planting: Innovative Approaches to Engage the Marketplace*. He is a frequent speaker on areas of church planting, evangelism, and marketplace mission. In addition to his role as a teaching pastor in a local church plant and church planting coach, Jay is an entrepreneur with a handful of small businesses. His hobbies include tree houses, axe throwing, and small business incubation. He can be contacted at: w@moons.com.

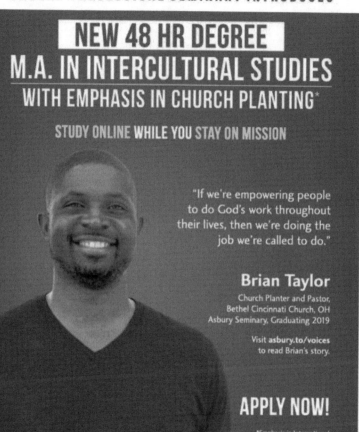

Resources for Practical evangelism In The 21st Century

PRACTICAL EVANGELISM
FOR THE TWENTY-
FIRST CENTURY

- Learn innovative approaches to evangelism
- Mobilize your church plant in evangelism
- Empower your team to "remove their fear and return to the story."

Hear what others are saying,

"It blends creativity and fun into a great time."

"It makes evangelism more fun and relaxing, so we don't feel so tense."

FIND MORE INFORMATION
AND RESOURCES AT
DIGITALBIBLECOLLEGE.COM
or contact w@moons.com

"I have used many different tools to prepare for evangelism and this is the best tool for engaging others."

EXPONENTIAL
RESOURCING CHURCH PLANTERS

- 90+ eBooks
- Largest annual church planting conference in the world (Exponential Global Event in Orlando)
- Regional Conferences - Boise, DC, Southern CA, Bay Area CA, Chicago, Houston and New York City
- Exponential Español (spoken in Spanish)
- 200+ Roundtables on Topics like Church Multiplication, Mobilization, Church Planting, Emotionally Healthy Leaders, The Future of the Church, and More
- Exponential HUB - Free Digital Platform offering content & conversation (multiplication.org/HUB)
- FREE Online Multiplication & Mobilization Assessments
- FREE Online Multiplication & Mobilization Courses
- Conference content available via Digital Access Pass (Training Videos)
- Weekly Newsletter
- 1000+ Hours of Free Audio Training
- 100s of Hours of Free Video Training
- Free Podcast Interviews

exponential.org

Twitter.com/churchplanting
Facebook.com/churchplanting
Instagram.com/church_planting

Made in the USA
Middletown, DE
16 February 2024

49915541R00076